The First American

Soccer Trivia Book

Jamie Clary

The First American Soccer Trivia Book

by Jamie Clary

Copyright©2007 by FreeFalling Graffiti
Hendersonville, Tennessee
All Rights Reserved
ISBN-13: 978-0-9744094-1-2
ISBN-10: 0-9744094-1-3

Library of Congress Control Number: 2007902086

Please direct all inquiries to
FreeFalling Graffiti
143 Cages Road
Hendersonville, TN 37075

Printed in the United States of America

Peg Brown is the woman at the National Soccer Hall of Fame who carries more history in her head and keeps more memorabelia at her fingertips than any aging soccer player will appreciate ever.

Hap Myers was a man from St. Louis who chronicled decades of soccer history without concern for the possibility that nobody would ever appreciate his work.

Barry Jones was one of my coaches and one of those Brits who carried football to the soccer fields of the American suburbs.

Derreck Bentley once offered me the #2 jersey in high school when he was too hurt to wear it.

This book is dedicated to them.

Contents

Pre-game

Which English colony was the location of the first known mention of soccer in the future United States?
Henry Spelman was an immigrant from England who came to the New World, more specifically the Virginia colony. He lived with other immigrants and with the Powhatan Indians, chronicling his life in a journal that was published in 1872. In the book, titled *Relation of Virginia*, Spelman wrote of a football game and making "gooles".

During what century was soccer first played in North America?
This is a tough one. It's not like Fisher-Price launched a soccer kit through Sears one day and Americans made it the top gift the following Christmas. The game likely came to our nation's shores before we were a nation via the country that we rebelled from. Most historians pick the year 1609 because of a depiction of a kicking game in Henry Spelman's *Relation of Virginia*. However, what was played in Virginia then was a make-it-up-as-we-go affair with a loose basis upon what was remembered from England. Soccer in the United States—and England—still had some refining to go through.

What North American city banned soccer in 1657?
Throughout the 1600s the game that was considered the forerunner of soccer often denigrated into a situation where something resembling a ball bounced along near something resembling a riot. Because of the violence, Boston banned the game and imposed a 20-shilling fine for offenders.

What word does *soccer* originate from?
We had all this confusion in the United States about rules during the 1800s. Actually the whole world was confused as well until England stepped in. The Football Association

of England formed in 1863 and laid out the rules for soccer,
thus differentiating for Americans and the rest of the world
what was soccer and what was not. More simply put, when
the Football Association of England wrote out a set of rules,
soccer games could be designated because the teams came
together to play under "association rules", thus playing
what became known as association football, often written
as *assoc* for short. English youth were fond of a slang that
added *ers* to words, thus modifying the game's name to
assoccers and then the shorter version, *soccer*.

What is the name of the global governing body of soccer?

More history of the game. I will be brief, and, no, this will
not be on the final exam. England created the game and
refined it. As the game grew in Europe, some other
countries saw the need to create an organization for play
between teams of separate nations. In 1904 France,
Belgium, Denmark, the Netherlands, Spain, Sweden, and
Switzerland formed *Fédération Internationale de Football
Association*, usually written as *FIFA* and pronounced *fee-
fah*.

Who is considered the father of American soccer?

When people dismiss soccer as having no history in the
United States, they discard a great deal of work by Thomas
W. Cahill. Born in 1864 in Yonkers, New York, Cahill
moved to St. Louis seven years later and participated in
soccer, baseball, and track. As an adult his life met a
crossroads while playing soccer for Christian Brothers
College in St. Louis. An opponent's criticism of his skills
incited Cahill to start his own team in revenge. He put
together the Shamrocks, spent $5,000 on players, and won
city championships in 1899 and 1900. Capitalizing on
those experiences, Cahill took a job with the A.G. Spalding
Company. There he became a promoter of athletics,

gradually concentrating on soccer. He coordinated the first tours of European teams to the United States and he organized the first team of U.S. players for a tour of Europe. In the meantime he organized the United States Football Association (which eventually changed its name to the United States Soccer Federation) as a means of nationalizing the sport in the United States. After he did that, Cahill traveled to Sweden to seek national recognition from FIFA. Receiving that, Cahill served as secretary of the United States Football Association for 13 years.

What statistic did the United States contribute to soccer?

In 1980 Gerald Eskenazi published *A Thinking Man's Guide to Pro Soccer*. He calls the assist an American concept. Regardless of who created it, Brandi Chastain appreciated it. From the time she was young through college, her grandfather paid her $1 for goals and $1.50 for assists. His point was that it was more important to become part of someone else's accomplishments.

When was the first game for the U.S. Men's National Team?

Getting into the semantics of the question, the answer could be 1885, when players from the American Football Association, a group of clubs from towns along the Hudson River, took on a team from Canada in East Newark, New Jersey. However, who's to say that some Indians did not cross the border before there was a border and have a pick-up game a few years earlier. To really put a date on the first national team game—one played by a team put together by the United States Soccer Federation—we would have to say 1916, when the USSF sponsored a tour of U.S. all-stars to Sweden and Norway. There we beat Sweden 3-2 and tied Norway 1-1.

**Who has been a part of FIFA longer—the U.S.,
England, or Mexico?**
After seven European nations formed FIFA without them in
1904, England responded by saying something like, "We
don't need your stinking rules." And they did it with a
British accent and probably substituted "stinking" with
"bloody". They saw the situation like Major League
Baseball would if El Salvador and the Dominican Republic
decided to write the international rules for baseball.
Anyway, England sat out of FIFA until 1906 but left twice
for more than 20 years. Mexico joined in 1929. The U.S.
has been part of FIFA continuously since 1913, giving us
more time as a member than the other two.

**Why wouldn't FIFA accept the United States as a
member in 1912?**
FIFA has a policy of recognizing one national organization
per country. In 1912 both the American Football
Association and American Amateur Football Association,
approached FIFA for acceptance to be anointed the
governing body of soccer for the U.S. FIFA rejected the
applications, telling representatives of both groups to work
out their differences. The amateur football organization
returned to form the United States Football Association,
pulling in other leagues and groups of teams, eventually
including the American Football Association as well.
When the United States Football Association approached
FIFA in 1913, it gained acceptance as a national body. That
foundation of being responsible for professional and
amateur play is greatly to blame for soccer's second-level
status as a sport in the U.S. For decades to come, the
United States Football Association (now known as the
United States Soccer Federation) concentrated on semi-pro,
immigrant-based, adult leagues. "The USFA completely
ignored college or high school soccer," wrote the authors of

Offside: Soccer & American Exceptionalism. Meanwhile high schools and colleges were exactly where football and basketball were flourishing. The USFA also retarded the growth of professional teams. Attracting financial interest became a difficult objective when potential investors realized that they would be governed by people not investing, explained a baseball writer in a 1927 issue of *Soccer Pictorial Weekly.* He then wondered what heights pro baseball would have reached "under the control of the Amateur Athletic Union."

Why did FIFA get involved with the election of the president of the United States Soccer Federation in 1990?

Peter Ueberroth, the president of the Los Angeles Olympic Organizing Committee, appointed Alan Rothenberg to be commissioner of the 1984 Olympic soccer tournament. Those matches were enormously successful in attendance and revenue. Some time after FIFA had chosen the U.S. to hold the 1994 World Cup, FIFA leadership became concerned that preparations for the 1994 tournament were falling behind. Remembering Rothenberg's abilities with the Olympics, FIFA Vice President Joseph Blatter suggested that Rothenberg run for president of the United States Soccer Federation in 1990 to lead the organizing effort for the World Cup and the construction of a U.S. professional league. Rothenberg won the election, became head of the World Cup, and led the launch of Major League Soccer.

What colors were on the official ball of the North American Soccer League?

Not only did the 32-panel ball stand out for its red stars, but it brought the world's game to the United States by being adorned in white and blue strips as well.

The NASL had its red, white, and blue ball. What made the ball used by the Major Indoor Soccer League stand out?
It was orange and brighter than a traffic safety cone.

What made St. Louis's NASL team stand out?
St. Louis was just as much a soccer hotbed as the East Coast was from 1880 through 1980. Pick-up games evolved into neighborhood challenge matches, and casual teams started signing players to contracts. The Thistles, Shamrocks, Hibernians, Saint Louis Amateur Football Club, and Western Football Association formed a league in 1886. As with teams on the East Coast, St. Louis soccer stemmed from immigrants. However, as those immigrants had children and the game spread through the city, the St. Louis clubs became more American. The Kensingtons, winners of the St. Louis city title in 1890 without giving up a goal, included only domestic born players. When the St. Louis Stars joined the NASL in 1967, the roster was dramatically different for the same reason. It was primarily made of American-born players while the other NASL teams were full of foreigners. The base of talent contributed to one local television station's decision to broadcast some of the Stars' games.

Compared to Europe and South America, there are three demographic differences in the people who play soccer in the U.S. What are they?
The progress of soccer has been retarded repeatedly when parents and coaches attempt to compete with other sports for playing fields. Soccer requires real estate. Between the oceans and the borders of the United States, the most difficult areas to find available real estate are the cities— lots of pavement, high-density buildings, and park space already sliced apart by football, basketball, baseball, and softball. Soccer, by virtue of its timing, grew in the

suburbs, where virgin land was available. The path of least resistance was in the suburbs. By contrast, players in Europe and South America usually came from the largest cities, having played in the streets. Also, U.S. suburbs are typically middle class and white; ergo soccer teams in the United States are disproportionately middle class and white. By contrast other nations find their players from the lower class and all races. That image of the American soccer player (suburban, white, and upper-class) is changing, however. "You're starting to see us attract greater diversity," said U.S. National Team Manager Bruce Arena in 2005. "It's not a white suburban sport anymore." Kids—especially minorities—will be more inclined to excel in soccer than in other sports as time passes. Arena noted the progress by acknowledging that in 1995 there were not 11 black players who were good enough to play on the national team. In 2005, he could put together a whole team of black players.

In 1968 Robert Guelker, president of the United States Soccer Federation, provided six objectives for the organization. How many of them focused on youth? One of the hindrances to soccer's growth in the U.S. has been that those who invest money in teams have been more interested in making money than building the game. Meanwhile, the people and organizations involved in building the game rarely have had enough money to do it. When the money side announced its goals for the future of the American Soccer League in 1954 they included new stadiums, increased attendance, better fields, televised games, a published brochure, and sponsorship of foreign team tours. Not a word about youth programs. With 14 years of hindsight, Robert Guelker gave his six goals for the organization charged with building the game. Objective number three was a larger office and more staff for the USSF. Not one of his six goals focused on youth. In fact

the word *youth* was not mentioned at all in his published
version of objectives.

Rules and Refs

**When Paul McSweeney, of St. Louis, ended his career as
a referee, what did he do with his whistle?**
After playing for Christian Brothers College, McSweeney
became nationally known as a top-level referee and even
received praise by a team of British players in 1905. When
a fight erupted between St. Louis's St. Leo's and the
Innisfails in a 1913 game, many of the 2,700 spectators
began rioting. McSweeney gave up the match, threw his
whistle over a nearby fence, and declared that he would
never officiate soccer again.

**How did the North American Soccer League change the
offside rule?**
With the game being so new to so many people in the U.S.,
a lot of media types chimed in with ways to Americanize
the game for greater fan appeal. Then and now we have
heard calls for larger goals, smaller fields, more subs, and
three points for kicking the ball over the goal. The NASL
addressed low scoring by creating a point system that
rewarded goals as well as victories and took aim at the
offside rule. The league used offside stripes from 1973
through 1981. In each half of the field, 35 yards from the
goal line, was a stripe running across the field. Instead of
using the half-way line to determine offside position, these
lines did the job, allowing teams to ignore offside in the
middle third of the field.

**Why did Franz Beckenbauer move from defense to
midfield after joining the NASL?**
In Germany Beckenbauer created the *libero*, or sweeper,

position that allowed the last defender to roam free of marking any opponents. The sweeper became the anchor of the defense and usually provided the voice that sent his team's defenders forward to catch opponents offside. Since his offside trap could push opponents up to the half-way line and since he was not marking an opponent, Beckenbauer made occasional runs toward his opponent's goal. However, in the NASL Beckenbauer's sweeper position had him frequently standing only 35 yards from his goal—at the offside stripe—while his team was attacking far up field. Getting into the attack as a sweeper involved longer runs and longer recovery. So Beckenbauer started playing midfield.

Why was referee Kurt Roethlisberger sent home before the end of the 1994 World Cup?
Roethlisberger was the center referee for the match between Germany and Belgium, a round-of-16 game. Germany was up 3-1, in the second half facing daunting pressure from Belgium. In the 70th minute Belgium's Josip Weber was assaulted like a World War II French border by two Germans in the penalty area. No call. Just before the final whistle Belgium scored to lose 3-2. FIFA General Secretary Joseph Blatter watched the play and decided that Roethlisberger would not be among the referees working the next rounds.

What illegal act did Brianna Scurry admit to after the penalty kicks in the final of the 1999 Women's World Cup?
Her coach, Tony DiCicco, had expressed to Scurry that saving a penalty kick virtually required that she move forward before the ball was kicked to decrease the shooter's angle. In that classic game, Scurry stepped out approximately three yards before the third shot was taken against her, enabling her to make the save. During a talk

show appearance after the tournament, Scurry said that it wasn't cheating since the referee did not call it. The referee later watched replays of the penalty kicks and said no call was needed. *Los Angeles Times* Sports Editor Bill Dwyre praised the team for its accomplishment and its impact on women and women's sports. However, he pointed out, "The U.S. cheated to win."

During the 2002 World Cup game between the U.S. and Mexico, what did John O'Brien do that could have dramatically changed the game's outcome had the referee seen it?

It's a funny question, I agree. However, with our slanted view of things, most Americans either never noticed or quickly forgot how fortunate we were with a no-call against Mexico. O'Brien leaped up in the penalty area against Mexico's Rafael Marquez during that game for a ball in the air. O'Brien went in with his whole body but knocked the ball away with his hand. Actually he punched the ball away. No call; no penalty kick. We won. Mexico went home.

What did German Torsten Frings use to prevent a U.S. shot from going into the goal during the United States' game versus Germany in the 2002 World Cup quarterfinals?

At the time, Germany was up 1-0. From a U.S. corner kick, a header went on to be volleyed by Greg Berhalter. The ball skipped past goalkeeper Oliver Khan and headed toward the net. Before reaching the goal line, though, the ball was turned back by Frings' outstretched arm. Khan then scooped it up. After the game Franz Beckenbauer said, "America was clearly the better team for 90 minutes." Some German players and television commentators agreed. Often they pointed out that the U.S. at least deserved a penalty kick to tie it.

How many U.S. National Team games did Taylor Twellman play in before scoring for the team?

Twellman was tearing up the nets of Major League Soccer when National Team Coach Bruce Arena called him up. There, he hit a skid, coming close a couple times but repeatedly short of his first international goal for the team. Against Trinidad and Tobago, in his tenth national team game, Twellman put one away, but the assistant referee incorrectly called offside. The same referee blew three corner kicks and a penalty kick in the game. Four games later Twellman scored one that stayed on the scoreboard. His injustice shares notoriety with bad calls on Alexi Lalas and Landon Donovan. Lalas was incorrectly called offside against Columbia during the 1994 World Cup. A goal was called back. Donovan was called for an offensive foul against Poland during the 2002 World Cup. His goal was disallowed as well. Less than a week after scoring his first goal for the national team, Twellman notched his 17th of the season in MLS, to give him the league's outright title of scoring leader. During a U.S. game in January 2006, Twellman scored three.

How many U.S. men have been ejected from games in the World Cup?

None of the members of the U.S. team in 1930 was ejected. That was true for 1934 and 1950 as well. Against Czechoslovakia in 1990, Eric Wynalda was sent off in the 57th minute. In 1994 Fernando Clavijo got sent off for his second caution in the 85th minute against Brazil. No U.S. player was ejected in the World Cups of 1998 or 2002. In 2006 Eddie Pope and Pablo Mastroeni were tossed in the game against Italy.

Who was ejected from the U.S./Mexico game in the 2002 World Cup?

In the 88th minute Mexico's captain Raphael Marquez gave

Cobi Jones a flying body block as Jones went up to play a ball in the air. Marquez was known as a physical player: he had collided with Brian McBride in a February 2001 World Cup qualifier, sending McBride off the field with a golf ball bulging from his head. For Marquez's foul on Jones in 2002 he was shown an immediate red.

How many cautions came out in that game?
A couple. Actually more than a couple. Among the 35 fouls there were 10 cautions, five for the U.S. and five for Mexico.

How many players have been ejected during MLS championship games?
Nobody had been ejected through the first eight editions of the final game. In the ninth MLS Cup, D.C. United's Dema Kovalenko was shown immediate red for a handball that denied an obvious goal scoring opportunity. Leading 2-0 at the time, D.C. held on to win 3-2.

Ken Aston is well known among upper level soccer referees in the United States for conducting many clinics. What tangible items did he contribute to soccer worldwide?
Prior to the 1970 World Cup, Aston noticed that the language barrier between referees and teams often caused confusion about players being booked. Television commentators were frequently in the dark as well. Aston, a top referee, had witnessed those problems during the 1966 World Cup and then noticed the similarities between traffic signals and referee actions. He decided that two cards could be displayed: a red oval for ejections and a yellow rectangle for cautions. His idea resolved the confusion among players and also made decisions more apparent for people watching on black-and-white televisions.

Through 2006 who of this list—Michelle Akers, Julie Foudy, Mia Hamm, Brianna Scurry, and Tiffeny Milbrett—has never been ejected during a women's national team game?
The first U.S. Women's National Team ejection was on Michelle Akers just prior to the 1991 Women's World Cup in a match versus China. Brianna Scurry got one during the 1995 Women's World Cup against Denmark. Prior to the 1999 World Cup, Julie Foudy was tossed out in a match against Brazil, and Tiffeny Milbrett received two cautions, thus an ejection, against Japan. Hamm is the only of the list to never see red as a women's national team member.

How many referees used whistles for the 2004 women's soccer final of the Athens Olympics?
No, there was no experiment with multiple whistles on the field simultaneously. However, two referees did use whistles that day. Referee Jenny Palmquist called the first 90 minutes, which had the United States and Brazil tied at one goal apiece. Then Palmquist told her referee teammates that she was unable to continue in the summer heat. Fourth official Dianne Ferreira-James took the center for overtime, where the Americans scored and won 2-1.

During the 2003 Women's World Cup, American Catherine Reddick scored two goals for her first time in a U.S.A. jersey, helping the U.S. beat North Korea 3-0. Why was she late getting to the airport after the game?
Drawn at random, Reddick, Julie Foudy, and two North Korean players were asked to give urine samples after the game. Foudy did fine, but Reddick, who could not provide a sample at first, went through 80 ounces of Powerade, cup after cup of water, and three hours while her teammates dressed, gave post-game interviews, and made their way to the Columbus airport. Reddick blamed stage fright as Foudy sang to her and drug-testing technicians made

suggestions. Waiting for Reddick, the chartered plane was
delayed by an hour before taking off for Providence, Rhode
Island.

U.S. on the World Stage

Who scored the first ever hat trick during a game in the World Cup?

Forward Bert Patenaude was credited with the first-ever
hat-trick in World Cup history, scoring all three goals in the
USA's 3-0 win over Paraguay on July 17, 1930, in
Montevideo, Uruguay.

Did the U.S. qualify for the second round of the 1950 World Cup?

After a 3-1 loss to Spain and a 1-0 victory over England,
the U.S. had a shot to move into the second round. A U.S.
victory over Chile combined with an England victory over
Spain would have created a three-way tie on top of the
group. Goals would be used to break the tie. After the U.S.
players lost to Chile and began to head home, some looked
back to the match against Spain as a wasted opportunity.
The U.S. had started well against Spain, scoring in the 17th
minute and reaching half-time 1-0. The lead was
maintained until late in the game, when the U.S. gave up
two goals. Walter Barr, one of the U.S. players, said in
2005 that he felt more disappointment in the team's loss to
Spain than the joy he felt from the victory over England.
He said, "We played a better game against Spain." Spain
went into the second round as the other three teams finished
each with one win and two losses. On goal difference, the
U.S. finished fourth, Chile third, and England second.

Was the 1950 U.S. Men's National Team really that bad? More specifically, of the U.S.'s previous 12

**international matches before meeting England in the
World Cup, how many did the U.S. win?**
According to records with the United States Soccer
Federation, the U.S.'s first three games after the 1934
World Cup were all against Mexico. The Mexico team
scored 19 goals to our 6 in those three losses. Then the
world went off to war, and Sylvester Stallone saved the
allies' pride (a reference that will be explained later),
allowing us to resume international competition in 1947.
We picked up where we had left off, with our southern
amigo, losing 5-0. We then lost to Cuba 5-2, to Norway 11-
0, Northern Ireland 5-0, and Scotland 4-0. We earned our
ticket to the 1950 World Cup with a 1-1 tie to Cuba and
later a 5-2 win over Cuba. In between those qualifying
games with Cuba, we dropped two more to Mexico by a
total score of 12-2. Our 12-game record going into the
1950 World Cup was one win, one draw, and 10 losses.

**How many years passed between the 1950 England
game and the next victory for the U.S. Men's National
Team?**
After the United Sates stunned the world by beating
England in 1950, U.S. Head Coach Bill Jeffrey said, "This
is all we need to make the game go over in the States."
Had he predicted doom for soccer in the states, he would
have been far more accurate. During 1952, 1953, and early
1954 we played and lost four games. We gained our first
post-1950 victory, over Haiti, in 1954. We beat Haiti a
second time in 1954 as part of qualifying for the 1956
World Cup. Then through 1966 it was bleak, real bleak.
With the Haiti victories included, we spent sixteen years
earning three wins, three ties, and 14 losses.

**After 1950, when was the next time the United States
played in the World Cup?**
As if England, the creators of the game, put a spell on us

for beating them in 1950, we entered the dark ages of U.S. soccer. The next time that the U.S. played in the World Cup was 40 years later, 1990.

Through 2006, the United States has sent teams to eight World Cups. The first five had at least one player from a particular city. Which city?
Whereas the East Coast often was the first home for immigrants, their sons and daughters frequently made the Mid-west their families' next stop. That additional step was enough to call them Americans but not too much to prevent them from learning the game their parents had grown up with. In addition to being a melting pot of people from Western Europe, St. Louis soccer thrived because of its Catholic culture. Priests in charge of the churches, schools, and recreational leagues tossed bats and footballs into closets. They understood soccer, so they taught soccer, putting the city level with the East Coast and decades ahead of any other city outside the Northeast. With such a quantity of players producing a higher quality of players, St. Louis was listed as the home town of World Cup players as often as Fall River, New York City, Bethlehem, and Newark. St. Louis had at least one player on each of the U.S. teams that played in the World Cups of 1930, 1934, and 1950. After a 40-year break from the World Cup, allowing other cities to add soccer to its sports repertoire, St. Louis still managed to stand out with players on the 1990 and 1994 teams. Harry Keough, a St. Louis native who played for the 1950 team, said that if he had grown up anywhere else, "I'd probably never have learned the game."

Why were Tony Meola, Kerry Zavagnin, and Josh Wolf dropped from the roster of the U.S. Men's National Team prior to a World Cup qualifier in 2004 against Grenada?
We could say it was Pablo Mastroeni's fault, but he could

blame his Colorado Rapids coach, Tim Hankinson. As Meola, Zavagnin, and Wolf worked out with Coach Bruce Arena and the U.S. Men's National Team, Mastroeni—who Arena also wanted in the national team camp—was kept by Hankinson, his coach, in Colorado. Hankinson was planning to release Mastroeni after a mid-week game against Kansas City. Arena, known for being a little blunt, delivered a message to Hankinson when he sent Meola, Zavagnin, and Wolf home from training camp early, allowing them to play for their club team. Their club team happened to be Kansas City, the team that Hankinson's Rapids would be facing. Arena said he was just being fair to both teams. All three of the Wizards played against the Rapids, and the Wizards won on a penalty kick by Wolf.

Which is the only nation to qualify for all 11 FIFA Under-17 World Championships prior to 2007?
The tournament was first played in 1985 as an under-16 competition but changed to under-17 for the 1991 version. It has been played every two years, and the U.S. has qualified for all 11 of them.

What's the best finish for the U.S. in the 11 FIFA Under-17 World Championships prior to 2007?
The U.S. finished fourth in 1999. Landon Donovan was awarded the golden ball. He and DeMarcus Beasley were named rising stars. Other members of the team included Oguchi Onyewu and Bobby Convey.

What has been the best finish for the U.S. in the Men's Under-20 World Cup prior to 2007?
Throughout much of the world, this is the most important international soccer tournament after the World Cup. Known officially as the FIFA World Youth Championship, it's a sign of talent to come. The first one was played in 1981. Every two years another one comes about. In 1989

the U.S. tied Mali, beat East Germany, and fell to Brazil—
good enough to meet Iraq in the quarterfinals, where we
won 2-1. In the semifinals the U.S. fell to Nigeria in extra
time and then lost the third place game to Brazil.
Regardless of the record (one draw, two wins, and three
losses), the U.S. brought home fourth place, its best finish
ever.

**During the 1989 FIFA World Youth Championship,
Steffen Karl played for East Germany against the U.S.
How did he become better known in 2005?**
Back in 1989, Karl was one of the East Germans whose
team fell to the U.S. 2-0. He is better known today for
being involved in game fixing in the unified Germany by
intentionally committing a penalty-kick foul in 2004 for
crooked referee Robert Hoyzer to call. Karl also offered
money to opposing goalkeepers in return for their pre-
arranged mistakes.

**Who was the youngest player of the 2003 FIFA World
Youth Championship?**
Freddy Adu, who had significant playing time, was 14-
years old at the time, the youngest to play in that
tournament. In the history of the World Youth
Championships, only one other person has played at a
younger age than Adu.

**Of the players who saw action on the U.S. under-20
team during the FIFA World Youth Championship in
1989, 12 were college-aged and four were young enough
to be in high school. How many were professionals?**
MLS's impact on soccer development may be no more
obvious than in the measure of the U.S.'s youth teams.
None of the 1989 players were professionals. By
comparison the 2003 and 2005 teams that went to the
World Youth Championships each included ten pros.

What nation won the first FIFA Under-19 Women's World Championship?

FIFA holds roughly 3,000 international tournaments for men, women, and children, the handicapped, and the feeble, indoor, on sand, and aboard aircraft carriers. Expecting readers to keep up with all those—even though 3,000 is an exaggeration—would be a little much. However, readers should be able to remember that this is a book on U.S. soccer. The U.S. won that tournament, the first under-19 world championship for women, by scoring 25 goals and giving up two to reach Canada in the tournament final. There, the U.S. won in extra time 1-0.

Prior to 2007 what has been the highest rank that the U.S. Men's National Team has reached among all FIFA countries?

The ranking system is based on points accumulated from international games with away games and more important games yielding greater points. College coaches and sports writers have no say. With a strong run into World Cup qualifying and a first-place finish in the CONCACAF Gold Cup, the United States reached number six in the world in July 2005. The only nations ahead of the U.S. were Brazil, Argentina, the Netherlands, Czech Republic, and Mexico.

1994 World Cup

What 1984 event led FIFA to choose the U.S. as host of the 1994 World Cup?

By far soccer games were the most successful events at the 1984 Summer Olympic Games, played in Los Angeles. In all, soccer competition brought in 1.5 million attendees, an average of 44,000 per game. For the gold medal match between France and Brazil, 101,799 people packed the Rose Bowl, leading FIFA to decide that the 1994 World

Cup could be successful in the United States even though the country had no strong history of the game and no true professional league.

Three major rule changes went into effect between the 1990 World Cup and 1994 World Cup. What were they?

The group the writes the rules for soccer, the International Football Association Board, heeded calls to liven up the game and changed two rules specifically to help out the offense. A player committing a foul to stop an obvious goal-scoring opportunity would be ejected. Prior to that the circumstance of the foul had no bearing on the decision of a referee to caution or eject a player. Also a player even with the second-to-last defender would no longer be in an offside position. The third change prohibited goalkeepers from using their hands when teammates passed the ball back to them.

How many times were players sent off for using fouls to deny obvious goal-scoring opportunities during the 1994 World Cup?

There are two schools of thought on this. Perhaps the new rule discouraged players from committing those "professional fouls". Or referees refused to hand out the punishment because of the severity. Either way, not one player was sent off under that rule during the tournament.

How many teams competed in the United States as part of the 1994 World Cup?

Qualifying for the 1994 World Cup started with 147 teams, vying for 24 spots. Those 24 teams came to the United States and were set in six groups of four. After playing the first round of games, all the first and second place teams from the groups were placed into the playoff round. Among the third and fourth place teams, the top four also went into the playoff round. The United States was the third place team in its group, good enough to get into the next round. Ever since, the final tournament has involved 32 teams.

During the 1994 World Cup, Germany beat Bolivia in the opening game. What World Cup jinx did Germany overcome with that victory?
Defending champions have always entered the tournament with an inordinate amount of attention, and in 1974 the defending champions entered the tournament by playing the opening game. It's a tradition that continues. The 1974 defending champion, Brazil, opened the tournament by tying Yugoslavia. In 1978 cup holders West Germany tied Poland. Argentina, winners in 1978, lost to Belgium in 1982. Italy tied Bulgaria in 1986. Argentina lost to Cameroon in 1990. Its 1-0 victory in 1994 made Germany the first defending champion in six tries to win the opening match.

Two of the players for Bolivia on that day ended up making big news in Major League Soccer in 1996. Who?
During that 1994 World Cup game Marco Etcheverry and Jamie Moreno came on as subs. At the time, Etcheverry was an international veteran and Moreno was a 21-year-old entering his first World Cup game. In 1996, they joined D.C. United, the team Etcheverry retired from eight years later after earning 101 career assists. All the while, Etcheverry's English proved to be as entertaining as his game. After MLS Cup '99, he commented on the hard surface of the field by saying, "The ball was bouncing around like bunnies."

Why didn't Diego Maradona play in Argentina's last two games of the 1994 World Cup?

The man had the world's eyes on him for his past successes and the weight of a nation with hopes for winning the 1994 World Cup. He had carried Argentina to the 1986 title with the goal of the tournament and the "hand of God". The cover of *Sports Illustrated* proclaimed him, trophy in hand, "the king of soccer." The king and his team reached the final of the 1990 World Cup but fell to Germany by one goal. His impact was more apparent after he left and then returned to Argentina's national team. Trying to qualify for the '94 World Cup without him, the team failed to win a direct spot from South America and had to beat Australia— with Maradona—to earn a berth. Once the tournament began, Maradona scored one goal in a 4-0 victory over Greece and led his team to a 2-1 victory over Nigeria. His team was becoming one of the favorites to win, and he was a darling of the media. At the end of that second match, though, Maradona's name was selected at random for drug testing, which led to the discovery of ephedrine, a banned substance. The story made network broadcasts throughout the U.S. and the world. His team, embarrassed and forced to play without him, won no more games. FIFA then imposed a 15-month, worldwide ban on him.

What team had a player who scored five goals in one game during the 1994 World Cup?
Oleg Salenko scored five times for Russia versus Cameroon in his team's last game of group play. Salenko's World Cup record for goals in a single game, however, had to share the spotlight with the guy who scored Cameroon's one goal. He was Roger Mila. At 42 years old, Mila set a record for being the oldest person to score a goal in the World Cup.

Why didn't Chile reach the 1994 World Cup that was played in the United States?
During Chile's attempt at qualifying for the 1990 World Cup, its goalkeeper and captain, Roberto Rojas, became

engulfed in smoke from a flare soon after his team went down 1-0 to Brazil in Brazil. When the wind made him visible again, Rojas could be seen on the ground with what appeared to be blood on his jersey. The Chile National Team walked off the field, claiming that the stadium was too dangerous for their players to continue and demanding a new game at a neutral site. FIFA investigated and determined that the episode was a hoax. Chile did not get a replay, Rojas was banned for life, and Chile was disqualified from the 1994 World Cup.

How far did England's national team go in the 1994 World Cup?

One of the greatest concerns, legitimate and overblown, about the World Cup being played in the United States was the hooligan element. For decades U.S. media had devoted much of their soccer coverage to overseas riots while riots were on the rise overseas. And on June 9, 1993, ABC's *World News Tonight* broadcasted a story about the likelihood of European fans inciting violence in U.S. cities during the 1994 World Cup. The source for so much of the violence seemed to be England, which began its final qualifying game by conceding a goal to San Marino nine seconds after the kick off. Even though England won that match 7-1, it did not advance from its qualifying group, which also included Poland and the Netherlands. And it did not make the journey across the pond to play in the tournament.

Who scored the goal that gave the United States a 1-0 lead against Columbia during the 1994 World Cup?

With Columbia on many people's short list of nations that could win the 1994 World Cup, the team was in a hole after losing its first game to Romania. Playing the U.S., Columbia's Andres Escobar slid to stop a pass. Instead he deflected the ball into his own goal to give the U.S. a 1-0 lead. Escobar's error proved costly when the final whistle had the U.S. up 2-1.

What misfortune befell Andres Escobar when he returned to Columbia after his team's ignoble departure from the 1994 World Cup?

With an extremely unsettling political environment in his home country, Escobar and his teammates returned to Columbia while the tournament was still progressing in the U.S. There Escobar was murdered, supposedly as restitution for scoring on his own team.

What spectacular play during the 1994 World Cup caught billionaire Phil Anschutz's attention and encouraged his investment in Major League Soccer?

It was the most seen near-goal of the tournament: Marcelo Balboa's bicycle kick during the U.S. match against Columbia. Video of Balboa's miss made many local news broadcasts and became a repeated highlight on national news broadcasts, showing casual observers and soccer detractors that ultimate soccer-specific effort. Phil Anschutz saw it as well, encouraging him to research the status of professional soccer and eventually to invest in MLS by buying into five teams. Ivan Gazidis, MLS deputy commissioner, explained the connection best in the *Rocky Mountain News* in 2003: "We might not have a league without Marcelo Balboa."

Who won the 1994 World Cup?

A month after the tournament's opening ceremonies involved Diana Ross failing to tap a ball into an open goal, the tournament ended with Italy and Brazil matching the singer's goal output during full time and extra periods. In the first World Cup Final to be decided on penalty kicks, Brazil beat Italy with a 3-2 shootout.

Women's National Team

In what year did the United States Women's National Team play its first game?
The United States Soccer Federation received an invitation for a women's team to play in a tournament in Italy in 1985. A representative of the U.S. Soccer Federation approached Mike Ryan during an Olympic Sports Festival in Louisiana to tell him that he had been selected as coach. Ryan, with 19-year-old Michelle Akers and an all-star team of players from the festival, led the U.S. team through four games in seven days. They lost and tied Denmark, lost to England, and lost to Italy.

Another big step for the U.S. women's team occurred a year later in Louisiana. What happened there?
The new coach for the U.S. Women's National Team, Anson Dorrance, got a call from a friend in Texas, telling him to take a look at a 14-year-old player named Mia Hamm. Dorrance, also the coach of the University of North Carolina women's team, scheduled a trip to see Hamm play in a tournament in Louisiana. Dorrance watched her play and added her to the national team a few months after she turned 15. Later he told Hamm that she could become the best player in the world.

Who's this? She was born in Selma, Alabama, with a club foot and had to sleep in corrective shoes while still young. When the U.S. Women's National Team coach first saw her, he felt she was too young to play for the national team. Her family moved around so much that they left her in the custody of her college coach while she was still 17 years old.
As the daughter of a U.S. Air Force colonel, Mia Hamm moved with her family to Italy soon after being born in Alabama. Her first soccer experience came there when she

was 18 months old, running through a park in her corrective shoes toward a man and his son who were kicking a soccer ball. She continued at the game while she was young, often competing with and against her older brother, Garrett. Moving frequently, Hamm's wedge into new schools and new neighborhoods was sports. Before entering college, she appeared with the U.S. Women's National Team, and she then led North Carolina to four straight NCAA Division I titles. Suffering from aplastic anemia, Garrett died in 1997. His sister praised Garrett for his tenacity and for never using her gender as a reason to exclude her.

What was the official name of the tournament that gave the Unites States women the world title in 1991?
Officially it was the FIFA Women's World Championship, as it was named in 1995 also. For the 1999 version, FIFA gave it the ultimate title of *World Cup*. Something else that was different about that first one in 1991 was that the halves were 40 minutes long.

What was the wacky experiment FIFA tried in the 1995 Women's World Cup?
With the games going 90 minutes instead of 80 minutes, FIFA decided that the women may need time-outs. The tournament rules allowed each team to call one, two-minute time-out per half. At first the opportunities for those breaks were not expressed well enough, requiring FIFA to clarify during the tournament that they could be called after goals and on a team's goal kicks and throw-ins.

During the 1995 Women's World Cup, the U.S. Women's National Team played its first and its last games against the same team. Which one?
The United States opened its group play with a 3-3 tie against China. The two teams each then played Denmark and Australia. Both then won their quarterfinal games.

When both teams lost in the semifinals, they found themselves meeting again, for third place. The U.S. prevailed 2-0. A day later Norway took first place over Germany.

During the 1995 Women's World Cup, China and the United States were set in the same first-round group. Who finished first in the group?

Finishing first in the group round provides a seemingly easier route in the knock-out round. On the race to win the group, the United States and China tied each other 3-3. The U.S. then beat Denmark 2-0 while China beat Australia 4-2. The best hope for the United States to win the group was by goal difference—beating Australia by a larger margin than China would beat Denmark. The problem was that the games were to be played simultaneously, leaving the target to be set and reset. Perhaps over-confident, the U.S. gave up a goal in the second half and found themselves trailing 1-0 before Julie Foudy scored the U.S.'s first goal. Meanwhile China and Denmark sat tied with 30 minutes left to play. All sorts of scenarios were plausible at that point, including the U.S. finishing third in the group. Then the U.S. took the lead with a Joy Fawcett goal, putting it first among the teams in the group at that moment. Receiving updates by mobile telephone, the players and coaches on the U.S. bench soon learned that China had scored, putting the two teams back in a tie for net goals but keeping China's edge on goals scored. Again the U.S. needed a goal to take first place in the group. Through 20 minutes nothing came. In stoppage time the Americans were awarded a penalty kick, and Carla Overbeck converted. But, the Chinese scored again as well, once again putting China ahead. Finally during the fourth minute of stoppage time, Debbie Keller ended the scoring for both games to put the U.S. up for good, 4-1 against Australia. By winning the group, the United States was set in a match against Japan, while China had to play Sweden, the host country.

Did the United States Women's National Team have to go through qualifying for the 1995 World Cup?
Unlike the rules for the Men's World Cup, the defending women's champion did not get a free pass to the 1995 Women's World Cup. The U.S., winner of the 1991 Women's World Cup, went through a qualifying tournament in Canada. With Canada, the Yanks won the two CONCACF slots to reach the World Cup.

During the 1999 Women's World Cup, the United States faced Nigeria in its second game. How many goals did Nigeria score?
During the second minute of the game, Brandi Chastain and Carla Overbeck collided, giving up the ball for a Nigerian player, who scored and gave her team a 1-0 lead. The U.S. promptly scored seven goals during the next 88 minutes.

Has the U.S. Women's National Team ever been involved in an on-field fight?
Anyone would guess that the men's national team has, and they would be correct. As for the women the only scuffle came on August 17, 1994, in a World Cup qualifying match against Trinidad and Tobago that was played in Montreal. Behind 11-1, the T&T players resorted to fouls of frustration, and one of them punched Carla Overbeck in the back of the head after Overbeck had passed the ball away. Overbeck replied with a couple punches of her own, knocking the aggressor to the ground. U.S. player Thori Staples met the flattened T&T player with a headlock, which was broken, leading to Staples taking a blow to her chin. A scramble ensued with more players joining in before Staples and the T&T player were ejected.

Prior to 2007, what is the largest margin of defeat for the United States Women's National Team?

Three times the U.S. women have lost games by three-goal margins. The most recent was a scoreless loss in 2003 to Germany. By the same 3-0 score, they lost to Canada in 2001. In 1998 the team fell 4-1 to Norway. The Norway game had a secondary competition going on that contributed to the U.S. loss. During practice the day prior, Shannon MacMillan and Julie Foudy had worked to outdo each other in nutmegging teammates. When the team reviewed the tape of Norway game two days later, Coach Tony DiCicco criticized both for particular plays that showed poor decisions. In front of DiCicco and the rest of the team, MacMillan and Foudy confessed that they were trying to nutmeg their opponents during the game.

Who is the career assist leader among U.S. Women's National Team players?

During her final national team game in December 2004, she set up two goals, ending her career with 114 assists during her 275 games for the United States. She's Mia Hamm. In that final game she sported a jersey with a different name, though. It had her married name, Garciapparra.

Which member of the United States Women's National Team is nicknamed Elvis?

During the media-filled days of the 1999 Women's World Cup, members of the U.S. team often checked into hotels under pseudonyms. Cindy Parlow, a native of Memphis, used Elvis. Michelle Akers used Pig Farmer, and Julie Foudy was Happy Gilmore.

Who is the youngest player ever to play in a game for the U.S. Women's National Team?

Two years before enrolling in college and at the age of 15, Mia Hamm played her first game for the United States

Women's National Team. She scored goals, handed out
assists, and kept earning spots on the team that repeatedly
won the biggest titles of women's soccer. At the age of 19,
she was the youngest member of the 91ers, the group of
women who won the 1991 Women's World Cup. She
started five of six games in the tournament and scored two
goals.

**Who was Amy Love and what did she have to do with
soccer in the United States?**
Love was the Jackie Robinson of Title IX. In 1975, three
years after Title IX had been passed, Love was chosen for a
travel team in California but was told later by the state
youth association that her gender forbade her from playing.
She sued under Title IX, received tremendous media
attention, and won.

Olympics

**What's the highest place that a United States men's
team has finished in the Olympics?**
The 1904 Olympic Games were coordinated with the
World's Fair, taking place in St. Louis. Soccer was one of
the competitions but was held as a club event. Invitations
went out to the club teams of the world. However, only
four accepted and only three made the trip: Galt Football
Club (Ontario, Canada), Christian Brothers College (St.
Louis), and St. Rose Parish School (St. Louis). They
finished in that order with U.S. teams taking silver and
bronze.

**During the 1996 Olympic soccer tournament, the United
States men opened their schedule against Argentina.
How long did it take the U.S. to score?**
The game was played in Birmingham, Alabama's Legion

Field, which has a sign inside: Football Capitol of the South. For decades the stadium hosted University of Alabama football and the fabled match-ups between Alabama and Auburn. When the U.S. soccer team started the game against Argentina, 83,183 fans were inside and were awarded quickly—in 36 seconds. Claudio Reyna celebrated his 23rd birthday by pounding in a volley off a deflection from 10 yards. The stadium now has an additional sign outside: Site of 1996 Olympic Soccer.

When was the first Olympic soccer competition for women?
The first men's competition was in 1900, and 96 years later the International Olympic Committee added women's soccer. Unlike the men's competition, the women's Olympic tournament involves national teams. Therefore, Olympic qualifying games and tournament games are considered national team appearances for the players.

How many times has the U.S. Women's National Team won the Olympic soccer tournament?
The first women's Olympic soccer tournament was played at the Atlanta Olympics in 1996. The U.S. women won it. They finished second in Sydney in 2000. In 2004 in Athens, the U.S. women beat Brazil in the final in overtime.

How many losses does the U.S. Women's National Team have in Olympic tournaments?
Through the 1996, 2000, and 2004 Olympic tournaments, the United States has played 16 games. Of those, the U.S. has won 12 and tied 3. The team's only loss came to Norway in the 2000 final.

How many times did the women's teams of the United States and Brazil play each other in the 2004 Olympic tournament?
The two teams met in their second games of group play, and the U.S. won 2-0. They met in the final as well, ending with a 2-1 overtime victory for the U.S. That double dose of one opponent actually has happened two other times to the U.S. Women's National Team during the Olympics. It happened in 1996 with China and again in 2000 with Norway.

Why have several women played for the United States in multiple Olympic soccer tournaments but only a few men have played in multiple Olympiads?
The obvious answer is that the U.S. men's teams have not qualified for every Olympic Games while the women have. That's true, but it's not the correct answer. The women's tournament is for national teams, allowing unlimited eligibility for women. For the men, the International Olympic Committee wrestled with two issues for decades: professionalism and conflicts with FIFA's World Cup competition. When the I.O.C. started allowing professionals, it did it haphazardly and inconsistently. For a time professionals from only Europe and South America were forbidden. At another time only Eastern bloc nations could use pros. Then FIFA stepped in to reclaim its ground as the body responsible for the highest international tournament and even threatened to ban its members from competing in the Olympics. As a compromise the I.O.C. agreed to limit the men's Olympic teams to players under 23 years old with three exceptions. Each team that qualifies for the Olympic tournament is allowed three overage players.

How many soccer games from the 1984 Summer Olympics were shown live by ABC?
With ESPN and ESPN2, both owned by the same company, ABC has become the top English-speaking soccer network in the United States, regularly showing national team games and MLS games. The three channels covered 52 games of the 1994 World Cup. However, back in 1984 ABC did not show any Olympic Games live, and the network caught hell about it.

Colleges

What college banned soccer in 1860?
For the same reasons that the city of Boston had banned the evolving game, Harvard faculty were leery of football/soccer/street brawling. They especially took notice of Bloody Monday, a phenomena where something resembling a sphere tumbled calmly nearby something resembling a crowd of students making mayhem. The mayhem was sophomores versus freshmen. "The ball . . . attracted little attention following the open kickoff," explained *The American Encyclopedia of Soccer*. After the 1860 version of the game/brawl, Harvard's faculty banned its return. The students promptly held a funeral and eulogized the game.

In what year was the first soccer game between colleges played in the United States?
The game of soccer was still so far from maturity that the match between Rutgers and Princeton on November 6, 1869, is considered the first intercollegiate soccer game as well as the first intercollegiate American football game. At the time, New England towns were playing variations and combinations of three games (soccer, the Boston game, and Rugby) that had differences in the number of players and rules concerning batting the ball, carrying the ball, tackling

players, kicking players, and means of scoring. The two
college teams drew up a set of rules just before the start,
and Rutgers won 6-4.

What St. Louis college was organizing leagues and teams in the 1890s?

With several of its students playing soccer, Christian
Brothers College provided a field for games and later
organized amateur, junior amateur, and parochial leagues
for non-students. The adult teams were part of the St.
Louis leagues, which had several venues within the city.

How many St. Louis area colleges won national titles in 1973?

ESPN's Sports Center leads us to forget that college sports
involves more than NCAA Division I teams. Often we
assume that the best teams in a sport are the ones in
Division I. And we tend to discount the NAIA altogether.
St. Louis soccer enthusiasts were happy to remind people of
those other classifications in 1973 when St. Louis
University won the NCAA Division I title, University of
Missouri-St. Louis won the NCAA Division II
championship, and Florissant Valley Community College
won the National Junior College Athletic Association title.
In addition to the three national championships held by St.
Louis schools, several St. Louis products contributed to that
season's NAIA title won by Quincy University, just a
couple hours north of St. Louis. The city had one
additional component that made it the U.S.'s soccer city in
1973. When Dan Counce was named the best college
soccer player, it gave St. Louis university players that honor
for the fifth consecutive season.

Why didn't St. Louis's two top college soccer teams play each other between 1899 and 1905?

When players and alumni of St. Louis University and

Christian Brothers College met in a rugby game in 1899, John Allen, of Christian Brothers, died as a result of the game. There were no rugby or soccer matches between the schools until a 1905 soccer game.

Where did Stern John play college soccer?
John's is a story of how skill, determination, and constant improvement can win out. Before John became Trinidad and Tobago's all-time leading national team scorer, he was playing for Columbus of Major League Soccer. With the crew, he was MLS's scoring leader as a rookie, and he scored 52 goals during the 1998 and 1999 seasons and playoffs. Before that he was playing for the New Orleans Riverboat Gamblers of the A-League. Previously he was playing college ball for Mercer County Community College in New Jersey.

How many members of the U.S. team that played in the 1990 Men's World Cup had played college soccer?
All of them. With a roster of 22, 19 had played in college, and three still were playing on college teams—Casey Keller, Chris Henderson, and Neil Covone.

Why did Julie Foudy decide to play soccer at Stanford University, a more expensive proposition, instead of at North Carolina?
Foudy, eventually the captain of the U.S. Women's National Team, had written in her journal as a fourth grader, that she had two goals: stop chewing her fingernails and earn straight A's for admission to Stanford. As a high school student considering several scholarship offers, she came across the journal and decided to keep at least the second resolution. Since Stanford did not yet offer women's soccer scholarships, Foudy's family paid for school.

What college has won the most men's NCAA Division I championships?

Among the colleges playing soccer when the NCAA started governing the game, St. Louis University was the head of the class. The school had an informal team in 1905 and played intramural games in the 1940s. After the university hired Robert Stewart, a former Syracuse University soccer player, as athletic director, the administration endorsed a club team in 1958 under Coach Robert Guelker. Pulling from the talent of many students who had played soccer locally, Guelker earned varsity status for the team in 1959, the first year of the NCAA's soccer championship tournament. His team won the post-season tournament that year and repeated in 1960. The SLU Billikens lost in the 1961 final but returned to win in 1962, 1963, and 1965. The team shared the 1967 title before winning it outright again in 1969, 1970, 1972, and 1973. The championship team of 1970 included a freshman class of 11, all from St. Louis. Dan Counce, one of the Billikens who won the title in 1973, was named the top soccer player in the nation that year and eventually became the general manager of the Colorado Rapids. Another player from that 1973 team was Dan Flynn. He became the general secretary of the United States Soccer Federation. St. Louis University's 10 titles are three more than Indiana's total.

Has any college ever won three men's NCAA Division I soccer titles in a row?

Seven times colleges have won back-to-back titles, giving each an opportunity to try for three straight. Only one time has a college succeeded. The University of Virginia won championships in 1991, 1992, and 1993. Then in 1994 it won again, for its fourth consecutive title.

Of the first 25 Women's NCAA Division I soccer championships (1982-2006), how many have been won by the University of North Carolina?
The Tar Heels are the undisputed leaders of women's college soccer. Its alumni list is a who's who of international stars. Altogether UNC has won 18 of the 24 Division I titles, including nine straight from 1986 through 1994. All of them have been under the coaching of Anson Dorrance.

Among the 24 Women's NCAA Division I soccer championships (1982-2005), which college has the most runner-up finishes?
North Carolina has three. So does Notre Dame. However, the University of Connecticut has four bridesmaid awards: 1984, 1990, 1997, and 2003. Had it not been for a wild 1990 semifinal, Connecticut would not have this infamous record. Late in that game that determined which team went to the final, Connecticut was down 1-0 to an undefeated Santa Clara University. With 10 seconds left, Connecticut scored on a 35-yard shot that squeezed past the goalkeeper. Neither team scored in overtime, sending the game to PKs. After five kicks, the two teams were tied at four each and headed into sudden death PKs. There Connecticut scored but Santa Clara missed, earning Connecticut a trip to another second-place finish.

Which colleges are tied for the second most Women's NCAA Division I championships?
With North Carolina winning all but seven of them between 1982 and 2005, Notre Dame and Portland are the only other schools to have won more than one each. Notre Dame took the title in 1995 and 2004. Portland won in 2002 and 2005.

What college team has the longest winning streak in college soccer?

The dominance of this team is amazing. We're talking winning streaks, which means that ties are no help. The women's team of the University of North Carolina won 92 games in a row between October 12, 1990, and September 30, 1994. The team also won 46 straight in 1997 and 1998, 36 straight in 1983 and 1984, another 36 in a row in 1986 and 1987, and 35 consecutively in 1994 and 1995. On top of that the program also holds the record for longest unbeaten streak, 103 games that ran from 1986 to 1990.

What coach has the most Division I NCAA women's team victories?

The actual number is unavailable because Anson Dorrance is still coaching at the University of North Carolina and still winning games. At the end of the 2006 season, he had 629 victories.

What coach has the most Division I NCAA men's team victories?

This is a long story, but it's one of those where fact is better than fiction. Jerry Yeagley, a physical education teacher, started coaching soccer at Indiana University in 1963 and turned it into a varsity sport in 1973. When the 2003 season neared, he was still at IU with five NCAA Division I titles and plans to retire at the end of the season. The NCAA record book had Yeagley at second in all-time victories, behind Stephen Negoesco, who had coached at the University of San Francisco from 1962 until 2000. The record book listed Negoesco as having 544 victories and Yeagley as having 527.

Needing 18 wins to pass Negoesco and going after another national championship, Yeagley was seeing both slip away early in his final go. The Hoosiers opened the schedule by beating California, but the season took an ugly turn right there with Yeagley 17 victories from the record. Everything that could go wrong pretty much did through the next eight games. Against UAB, Indiana played two overtimes but could only tie. They tied Georgetown as well by giving up two goals in the final five minutes. Then the Hoosiers lost by one goal to Connecticut and then to Akron by one goal in overtime. They got a 3-1 win against Fresno State but then lost to Notre Dame on a mis-hit shot that deflected off the butt of an Indiana defender in overtime. Then came Michigan State, 0-30 all-time versus Indiana. Indiana tied 1-1. Against Butler, another tie. In between the two ties was a game against Penn State. Indiana had a two-goal lead when lightning sent the teams off the field and nullified everything.

After nine games, Yeagley's Hoosiers had two wins, three losses, and four draws. It was the program's worst start in history. One of his players later told a *Soccer America* reporter that Yeagley said to them at that point, "Maybe I stayed one year too long." For the NCAA record, which he had said was not important to him, he was at 529 victories, still 16 away. To win another national championship and to reach 545 wins, Yeagley's team would have to win just about every last game of the schedule and stay unbeaten through post-season tournaments. Both looked so far from reality that players quit thinking about them. But if the first part of the season was how everything could go wrong, the rest of it was about how everything could go right.

On October 5, the team came from one-goal down to tie Michigan and then win in overtime for victory number 530. They then beat Wisconsin and Northwestern for victories 531 and 532. By the slimmest margin of 1-0, the Hoosiers beat Indiana University-Purdue University Indianapolis for Yeagley's 533rd victory. The 534th victory came against Ohio State. Ranked 24th on October 24, the Hoosiers beat fifth-ranked St. Louis for the coach's 535th win. They then beat Louisville—536. Against Kentucky, they had another squeaker but won 1-0 for number 537.

Playing Penn State without lightning or the 2-0 lead,
Indiana went into half-time behind 2-0. The game finished
3-2, and Yeagley had victory number 538, still seven shy of
a new all-time record. In the Big Ten tournament, Indiana
beat Wisconsin again, this time 1-0, to bring the quest down
to six victories. Then came the tournament final, pitting
Indiana against Penn State again. The two teams went 1-1
into a penalty-kick tie-breaker. The Hoosiers won.

        Technical questions about numbers and victories
then arose. The shootout win prolonged the Hoosiers'
season, but it counted as a tie in the official record book.
Yeagley still needed six more wins. However, the season,
at best, had only five games remaining, meaning that
Yeagley could hope for no better than a tie in all-time
victories. Nonetheless, achieving that tie would mean
another national championship. Any loss would end the
season, the quest for another championship, and the run at
becoming the top Division I coach. The Hoosiers next took
on Kentucky, needing overtime for a 2-1 victory. The
overtime winner was scored by Greg Badger, his first
college goal. Then there was Virginia Commonwealth, a 5-
0 win.

        Again technical concerns about numbers came up.
Prior to the Virginia Commonwealth game, Indiana
University and the NCAA believed that Yeagley was at 540
wins and that Negoesco had finished his career with 544. A
pre-game IU press release stated, "If the Hoosiers collect
the four wins necessary to capture the NCAA title, Yeagley
would match the 544 career wins." But David Woods, a
reporter for the *Indianapolis Star* noticed something. He
realized that San Francisco University's 1978 NCAA
championship had been vacated, or taken away, due to
Negoesco's use of an ineligible player through the
tournament. Along with the trophy, San Francisco
University also should have given up the four victories of
the 1978 tournament. Woods contacted the NCAA

statistics folks about the error. The NCAA checked its math, corrected the record book, and contacted Indiana University to tell Yeagley that his team's recent win, Yeagley's 541st, over Virginia Commonwealth had put him ahead of Negoesco. Good news: you have the record. Bad news: your team just loss some motivation as it prepares to face the defending national champion.

Every game could have been Yeagley's last. UCLA took an early lead against Yeagley's team. But Indiana tied it with a goal that found the net after a deflection. Indiana's second goal came from a shot that hit the crossbar and the goalkeeper before landing at Pat Yates' feet. He knocked it in and sent the Hoosiers into the semifinals. In the semifinals they went 0-0 through 90 minutes with Santa Clara. They played one overtime and were still scoreless. Then in the 104th minute, Yates put one in, giving Indiana a 1-0 win and a berth in the finals. Ycaglcy stood on the threshold of ending his career as the coach of a national champion.

Throughout the NCAA tournament, Yeagley had suffered from his own success. In recruiting and building strong players, the coach found himself without two of his best, Ned Grabavoy and Drew Moor. Selected for the Under-20 U.S. Men's National Team, they were in the United Arab Emirates playing in the Under-20 World Cup. Neither one had departed for the Under-20 tournament certain that their college team would still be playing when they would return in mid-December. However, after the United States got knocked out by Argentina on December 12th, the two Hoosiers started a long trek back to the United States hoping to make the final match on December 14th. In Germany, the two faced a decision when their flight was overbooked. Moor told Grabavoy to go on without him, and Grabavoy reached Columbus the night before the game. Moor eventually caught up, arriving in Columbus two hours before kick-off. Both started in the championship game, and in the 16th Minute, Grabavoy scored. Four minutes later Jacob Peterson scored. Indiana led 2-0 at half-time and held on to win 2-1 over St. John's. Yeagley earned victory number 544 among 101 defeats and 45 draws. He is now listed atop all other Division I coaches in total victories. The same list has Negoesco in second with 540 victories.

If there is one more facet that makes this a hard-to-believe story, throw in the situation with Todd Yeagley, the coach's son. The school's five previous titles had been won in '82, '83, '88, '98, and '99. Todd played at the school from '91 through '94, never winning a national championship with his father. Coach Yeagley told *Soccer America* that he always had been disappointed that none of the title-winning teams included his son. After leaving IU, Todd went on to play in MLS before returning to be an assistant coach with his dad. As an assistant in 2003, Todd embraced his dad after the championship game, noting that they had finally won a title together. The older Yeagley said, "The stars and the moon and everything aligned."

Where did Jerry Yeagley play his college soccer?
Yeagley played at West Chester University in Pennsylvania, where he helped the team win the NCAA soccer title 2-0 over St. Louis in 1961.

Among Illinois colleges, which one has won the most NCAA Division I men's soccer titles?
Actually there has been only one NCAA Division I title won by an Illinois College. It was won by the University of Southern Illinois at Edwardsville in 1979. The school is within sight of St. Louis. Bob Guelker was the SIUE coach in 1979, but had previously coached the University of St. Louis to Division I titles in 1959, 1960, 1962, 1963, and 1965. Between coaching St. Louis and winning the 1979 Division I title, he won a Division II title with SIUE. There

are a handful of coaches who have won titles in two divisions. However, Guelker remains the only coach to win Division I titles with two different colleges.

How many NCAA Division I championship games did the UCLA men's team play in before it won a title?
The UCLA men's team reached the championship games of 1970, 1972, and 1973 only to lose each time to St. Louis University. When UCLA reached the final in 1985, it faced American University. The two teams played without a goal for 90 minutes. After two overtimes, the score was still 0-0. After two more overtimes, the score was still unchanged. Two more, 0-0. The seventh, still. Finally, the eighth overtime yielded a UCLA goal. Three years prior the final had gone to eight overtimes as well. But UCLA's goal after 166 minutes, 5 seconds is still a record for time in an NCAA Division I soccer championship match.

Other Sports

In 1912 Dwight F. Davis, the parks commissioner of St. Louis, worked with local teams to provide city parks for a citywide soccer league. How did Davis make a name for himself in another sport?
Davis's help in reserving space in four city parks enabled the beginning of the Municipal Amateur Soccer League of St. Louis. This was the organization that put St. Louis in the center of the map for U.S. soccer for decades to come. Growing from the original 18 teams, the league added a junior division and was up to 2,000 players on 15 fields by 1924. During the season that ended in 1928 1.1 million fans came out to watch games. Sunday matches, especially the season-ending championship games, were bringing thousands of spectators out for free or cheap entertainment during the Great Depression. The municipal league became

a feeder for the professional league of St. Louis while also establishing teams for grammar and high school students. Davis went to become Secretary of War under Calvin Coolidge and governor general of the Philippines. He also served as president of the U.S. Lawn Tennis Association. His name is best known for what he did right out of college, though. Soon after his college tennis days at Harvard, he bought a trophy and invited Great Britain to send tennis players to compete as a team against his team of U.S. players. It was the first competition for the Davis Cup, which, since 1900 has developed into the international team competition for tennis sought every year among nations.

Which club team contributed the most members to the United States Men's National Team that went to the 1930 World Cup?
Jimmy Douglas, Jimmy Gallagher, and Bart McGhee were from the New York Nationals, which was owned by Charles Stoneham, who also owned the New York Giants baseball team. It was quite common for owners of major and minor league baseball clubs to own teams of the American Soccer League, which was the league the Nationals played in.

What evidence did ABC television provide in the 1970s that soccer players are better athletes than participants of other sports?
The network began its "Superstars" competition in 1973, matching up Americans from several sports to determine which of them was the best overall athlete. Keep in mind that this was during the big-three era of team sports, when participating in anything else—say soccer—could earn a person the label as being not tough enough or good enough in baseball, football, and basketball. Soccer was not "a real sport" in the minds of some. And it was the sport of communist nations. During 1974, the second year of "Superstars", soccer player Kyle Rote Jr. took first place.

Competing against Pete Rose, Reggie Jackson, Jim Palmer, O.J. Simpson, John Havlicek, Franco Harris, Stan Smith, and other top athletes, Rote showed the nation that soccer players were athletes, not just big-three rejects. In trying to repeat the feat in 1975, he finished third, but placed first again in 1976 and in 1977.

What professional team did Kyle Rote Jr.'s Father play for during most of his career?

It was not a soccer team. The older Rote was an All-American half-back (the American football type of half-back) from Southern Methodist University. Kyle Rote Sr. was the first overall draft pick of the National Football League—chosen by the New York Giants—in 1951. He went on to play 11 seasons in the league, making appearances in four pro-bowls.

Henry Davis, of Dallas, Texas, had an uncle in Tennessee. How did that change American soccer?

Henry Davis met Kyle Rote Jr. within a few days of the Rote family's relocation to Dallas. Henry and Kyle became good friends as they participated in athletics, including soccer. When Rote accepted a football scholarship to Oklahoma State University, Davis headed to Sewanee University in Tennessee. When Rote decided to leave college football and O.S.U., he went to join his good friend, who was playing soccer at Sewanee. Why had Davis chosen far-off Sewanee for a college education? His uncle was on the faculty there.

Who often competed with Pele as the most recognizable person on the planet?

We know Pele for playing in New York, the media center of North America and a global hub of commerce. We tend to forget that he also is the only player to have won the World Cup as a player three times, two of those on European soil.

And we can't forget that he first had a career on a South
American team that toured the world. He was so popular
that during a 1967 war among Nigerians, fighting stopped
in order for men of both factions to watch him play. When
Pele moved to New York to restart his career, Muhammad
Ali was defending boxing's heavyweight championship.
Ali fought in Europe during the 1960s, in Japan in 1972,
Indonesia in 1973, Africa in 1974, and Malaysia and the
Philippines in 1975. Tony Banks, a former minister of
sports in England, said that Pele had achieved the fame of
Ali, the most famous person in the world. Umbro's Peter
Draper said Pele lacked Ali's arrogance but measured up
with Ali in overall status. Author Harry Harris wrote that
Pele's fame was still growing as he was becoming "more
influential, more popular, more famous, and more
legendary" even though his best playing days were behind
him.

**What union sued Major League Soccer on behalf of the
league's players?**
Acting on behalf of the players of Major League Soccer, the
National Football League Players Association filed suit
against Major League Soccer in February 1997, accusing
MLS of violating anti-trust laws. MLS teams competed on
the field but deferred to the league when it came to
compensating players. There were no bidding wars
between teams for players. The NFL players wanted that
centralized pay structure outlawed, fearing that the NFL
could go the same way since the NFL's revenue sharing
plan was just a hair away. Nevertheless, the players lost the
suit, allowing the league to continue negotiating pay as one
structure, not several competing teams.

**Who was the special guest that traveled with U.S. Men's
National Team as it attempted to qualify for the 1990
World Cup?**

Nearly forty years after he had helped the United States beat England in the 1950 tournament, Walter Bahr traveled with the players who were trying to end the drought and qualify once again for the World Cup. During that drought Bahr had raised three sons: Casey, Chris, and Matt. They all played in the NASL. Chris, the 1975 rookie of the year with the Philadelphia Atoms, and Matt later joined the NFL. Both earned Super Bowl rings.

What sports-related event had Americans glued to their televisions on the night that the 1994 World Cup began?
Minutes after Germany dropped Bolivia in the opening game of the 1994 World Cup and less than 24 hours before the American team took on Switzerland, O.J. Simpson led California police officers on his low-speed chase. Earlier in the day instead of broadcasting the opening ceremonies from Chicago, ESPN had reported that Simpson would be charged with two murders.

Who was the kicker for the Miami Dolphins when they won Super Bowl VII?
The answer to this question provides a high and low for soccer in the United States. Garo Yepremian had come into the NFL in 1966, beginning the true conversion from kickers who hit the ball straight on with their toes to the ones who approached kicks from the side and met the ball with their laces. He ended his career as the scoring leader for the team, setting a standard of success in field goals and extra points that had other teams looking for their own soccer-style kickers. He is best known for playing with the undefeated Dolphins in 1972 and into the Super Bowl, where the Dolphins finished their perfect run. During that game, though, Yepremian, who had played soccer in England, gave the highlight reels something that forever had big-belly soccer enemies guffawing about the superiority of football players over every other athlete,

especially soccer players. After Yepremian had a field goal
blocked, he scampered to pick up the ball, and cocked his
arm to throw a pass downfield. His follow through not
only gave the impression that Yepremian had used the
wrong arm for the pass. It lacked the ball. The ball had
wobbled out of his hand and landed behind him for a
Redskins' player to run back for a touchdown.

**How did indoor soccer add a new dimension to
American football?**
With executive experience in the National Football League
and the United States Football League, James Foster
noticed arenas filling empty dates by hosting indoor soccer.
Working with some of the same arena managers and some
different ones, Foster started a league for indoor American
football in 1987. He served as commissioner of Arena
Football League and later led the creation of Arena Football
League 2, a farm system.

**In 1894 the American League of Professional Football
Clubs became the first professional soccer league in the
United States. What other sports background did the
owners of the teams have in common?**
The six teams were all owned by men who also owned
teams of baseball's National League. The soccer league,
lasting only through October of 1894, was a vehicle to
generate revenue from idle baseball parks.

**St. Louis's Busch Stadium recently was replaced with a
new stadium of the same name. What happened on the
site of the original stadium on November 24, 1881?**
The important thing here is the year because Busch
Stadium—formerly Sportsman's Park—was an empty lot in
1881, allowing it to host the first known soccer game in St.
Louis. Long before the stadium was built, the Athletic
Club and Mound City played soccer there. The city's

interest in soccer continued to grow it into the center of soccer activity of the country. Among the factors that contributed were an immigrant influence, moderate winter weather, rivalries among Catholic organizations, support from businesses, and baseball as the only other embedded professional sport in the city.

What logical event was scheduled to follow that game?
The Saint Louis Browns and Cincinnati Reds planned to play baseball after the soccer game. It would have been one of the first games of the new American Association of Baseball, formed just 22 days earlier in St. Louis. Unlike the National League, the American Association allowed Sunday games and drinking in the stands. Had the game not been cancelled due to cold weather, it also would have been one of the first ever for the St. Louis Browns, the team that became the St. Louis Cardinals.

What did the Brooklyn Dodgers do in 1957 that helped the International Soccer League?
After the Dodgers moved to Los Angeles in 1957, Ebbets Field was torn down. Several of the fixtures from the Ebbets Field lights were donated to the parks department of New York City. When the International Soccer League needed lights for its games at Downing Stadium on Randall's Island, the parks department installed them in 1963 with the understanding that the ISL would be a long-term tenant. The lights allowed larger crowds and more games in the stadium.

Where is the United States Soccer Hall of Fame?
The staff of the hall of fame says that the question they hear the most is "Why is it located in Oneonta, New York?" Oneonta State University and Hartwick College, both located in Oneonta, have had quality soccer programs for a long time, and the National Baseball Hall of Fame, located

in Cooperstown, is just a short trip away. The baseball hall of fame had long shown the impact a tourist destination could have when, in 1977, Hartwick won the NCAA Division I national soccer championship. Wondering where Hartwick's name would be enshrined for its accomplishment, Oneonta residents asked, "Where is the National Soccer Hall of Fame?" Oneonta Mayor James Lettis appointed Parks and Recreation Director Albert Colone, to find the answer. He found that the national soccer hall of fame was a storage room in Philadelphia. A task force including John D. Biggs, Bill Atchinson, and Jim Ross found that the Philadelphia Old-timers Association had established a hall of fame in 1950. Working together, the two groups established a physical location at Oneonta State University in 1979 and gained recognition by the United States Soccer Federation in 1983.

Among all the players to have played in the National Hockey League, Major League Baseball, the National Football League, the National Basketball Association, and Major League Soccer, who is the youngest to win a league championship?
Just as the 2003 Major League Soccer season ended, the league signed Freddy Adu to start playing for D.C. United in 2004. During half-time of MLS Cup '03, Adu made an appearance on national television and said that he hoped to be playing in the next championship game. He did. In the 65th minute of MLS Cup 2004, Adu, at 15 years old, went in as a substitute for D.C. United. United won the game 3-2.

Pop Culture

What side did England support during the U.S. Civil War?
What does that have to do with soccer? Since Great Britain

supported the Confederacy, says Christopher Merrill, author, of *The Grass of Another Country*, the next 60 years of U.S. society grew to shun British games in exchange for Yankee ones. The period, 1870 to 1930, was when our society of today really took shape, say authors Andrei S. Markovits and Steven L. Hellerman. They wrote *Offside: Soccer and American Exceptionalism.* That period also was when our "sport space" developed. The sports that were at the top of our national conscience in 1930 stayed at the top for the rest of the century. Soccer was not part of the sport space by 1930 because of the Civil War. It continued to be excluded, say the authors, because "it was virtually impossible" to add a sport to the U.S.'s sport space through 2000.

What two well-known singers partially owned the North American Soccer League's Philadelphia Fury?

In the 1970s pro soccer was a fad in the vein of disco. Especially on the East Coast and the West Coast, NASL games were the places to be seen for celebrities and people who wanted to be celebrities. So owning a team drew top attention, leading Peter Frampton and Paul Simon to buy into the Fury. They were owners in 1978, 1979, and 1980. Then the team was bought by Molson Breweries and moved to Montreal.

What New York restaurant hosted Pele and the Cosmos for their announcement that Pele was joining the team?

Perhaps nothing says trendy in New York as much as the "21" Club. Since soccer was a really just a trend in the mid-1970s, that's where the announcement took place on June 11, 1975. The king of soccer signed a contract for something near $4 million for three years. Aside from his salary, one of the items that came up during the press conference was that one detail had not been worked out: who would pay Pele's league registration. Asked directly at

the event, Cosmos President Clive Toye handed Pele the
fee, $15.

**One of the original Major Indoor Soccer League teams
was the Cincinnati Kids. Who was its famous co-
owner?**
Playing the first-ever MISL game on December 22, 1978,
the Kids drew over 10,000 people to Riverfront Coliseum
for their game against the New York Arrows. Pete Rose,
former component of the Big Red Machine and partial
owner of the Kids, ceremonially kicked out the first ball.

**Who of these people did not play soccer growing up:
Shaquille O'Neil, Cal Ripken Jr., Chelsea Clinton, or
Terry Bradshaw?**
Shaq talked about soccer on a talk show once, saying he
had to quit playing because he ended up kicking other kids.
Ripken played for Aberdeen High School in Maryland, and
Clinton played in Arkansas and D.C. Instead of playing
soccer, Bradshaw, known for playing a game that involves
butt-hugging pants, has often ridiculed soccer players for
their uniforms.

**What English singer was part owner of the Los Angeles
Aztecs?**
He also was on the board of directors for England's Watford
Football Club but was better known for "Rocket Man".
He's Elton John, and he loves men in shorts.

**Who played Billy Campbell in "Melrose Place" from the
first through 199th episodes?**
Who cares? Well, it was a big deal for soccer in this
country once upon a time, specifically in 1996. "Melrose
Place" had begun airing weekly in 1992 with Andrew Shue
playing Billy Campbell. When Major League Soccer was
taking shape, Shue expressed interest in playing for the Los

Angeles team. He had been an all-conference player at Dartmouth, where he had graduated in 1989. MLS execs and Galaxy staff saw the opportunity to assist their marketing efforts with a Hollywood celebrity while the coaching staff claimed that Shue's evaluation would be based solely on his soccer ability. He made the team and brought some exposure to the new-born league with appearances that included a guest spot on *Late Show with David Letterman*. During the season he played in five games for a total of 96 minutes, assisted on one goal, watched his team give up a 2-0 lead in MLS Cup '96, and was slapped four or five times by clothing-challenged actresses on the series' set. Shue did not return to the team for 1997 but continued on the show until 1998.

What was the name of the movie that starred Pele, Sylvester Stallone, and Michael Caine playing soccer during World War II? (Bonus points for the movie's European title.)
The movie was directed by John Huston, filmed in Hungary, and based on a real-life series of games played during the war. In the United States it was released in 1981 with the title *Victory*. In Europe it was known as *Escape to Victory*. In terms of Stallone's career, the movie hit theaters between *Rocky II* and *Rocky III*, (the movie in which Rocky first earned the title and the movie in which he loses and then regains the title against Mr. T's character, Clubber Lang).

What well-known college soccer coach suggested to producers that they make a movie about the 1950 U.S. World Cup team?
Angelo Pizzo, the producer of *Rudy* and *Hoosiers*, was in Bloomington, Indiana, where he happened to run into Jerry Yeagley, Indiana University's soccer coach. Pizzo asked Yeagley if there were any soccer stories worthy of making a

movie about. They talked about the 1999 U.S. Women's
World Cup victory and then Yeagley mentioned the surprise
victory by the U.S. men over England in the 1950 World
Cup. Pizzo and director David Anspaugh did some
research and found that there was a book about the game
written by Geoffrey Douglas, *The Game of Their Lives*.
Using the book's title, they made the movie and released it
in 2005.

**Who said about soccer in a 1981 movie, "This frigging
game is wrecking my life."?**
In *Victory*, the movie about a World War II soccer match
between the German National Team and Germany's
prisoners of war, Sylvester Stallone becomes the hero.
Initially he works to escape alone, thumbing his nose at the
recreation of other prisoners. His character shouts, "What
kind of game is this? For old ladies and fairies!" When his
escape becomes dependent upon the freedom of the soccer
team, though, Stallone has to play the game. Then his plan
to escape with the team is thwarted by footballers who
yearn for victory more than freedom. He secures a draw for
the allies by saving a penalty kick, and he dances a goal-
line jig just prior of the final whistle. The actions, probably
more the save than the jig, incite the crowd to rush the pitch
and deliver the team to safety. The movie proves the slim
impact the U.S. has had on international soccer. The lone
American on the allied team, Stallone's character, works his
way onto the team not with skill. In fact when his freedom
becomes tied to the team's escape, he utters words that are
fit for few actors and few nationalities: "This frigging game
is wrecking my life."

**Robert Duvall starred in the 2005 movie *Kicking and
Screaming*. Previously, though, he worked with Michael
Keaton in another soccer-themed movie. What was its
title?**

The movie actually was known under three titles but had the name *A Shot at Glory* when it was released in limited theaters in the United States in 2001. The alternative titles were *The Cup* and *Road to Glory*.

In that movie, actor Cole Hauser played an American on the team coached by Duvall's character. What position did Hauser play?
A Shot at Glory, as far as a sports movies go, is not as formulaic as most soccer films. The American character, however, is the predictable type. In the model of *Victory*'s Sylvester Stallone, Hauser plays the goalie. Without the two-run homer or the three-point field goal, soccer movies have always stumbled with a simple resolution to climactic suspense. The dramatic resolution in *Victory* came from Stallone's heroic penalty kick save to preserve a draw. Hauser, too, saves a penalty kick in *A Shot at Glory,* really doing no more than keeping his team alive.

What common co-star do the brief film careers of wrestler Hulk Hogan and soccer great Bobby Moore have in common? Bobby Moore, captain of the England National Team that won the 1966 World Cup, starred in *Victory* with Sylvester Stallone. Hulk Hogan starred in *Rocky III*, released just a year after *Victory*, which, of course also starred Sylvester Stallone.

The soccer game in *Victory* was based loosely on a series of games during World War II. It was dead on with what fact about matches between the national teams of Germany and England?
From a marketing perspective, *Victory* sought to take advantage of North America's soccer fascination in the late 1970s. It set Sylvester Stallone, the flag-waving Rocky Balboa, in World War II within the genre of Yank-saves-the-day. For a war movie in which the fighting is officiated

on a 1940s soccer field, an American hero requires a historically hazy premise and a slow-motion scene of strong, bare, white hands. The game initially is to be between prisoners of war and German troops from a nearby base. But with the words "We have never beaten England," German officers raise the importance of the game to full international status for propaganda purposes. They bring in the German National Team to play the best prisoners the allies—mostly British—can gather. The set-up is historically accurate. In 1930 England and Germany met for the first time, tying 3-3 in Berlin. The former and future military enemies met again in 1935; England won 3-0. England beat the Germans again, in 1938, 6-3. The two did not see each other another time before war broke out. Therefore, the movie's competitive premise is accurate: Germany, with two losses and a draw, had never beaten England prior to World War II.

The King

What is Pele's first name?
He was the savior of American soccer, the king of football, and the only person to win three World Cups as a player. He's best known as Pele, but his birth certificate says Edson Arantes do Nascimento.

What does *Pele* mean?
The man himself has no idea. He picked up the nickname when he was young and playing soccer in the streets. He fought the name for some time before accepting it. He has several theories—a combination of words from Turkish and Portuguese, a mispronunciation of an older player's name, a modification of the Portuguese word for foot—but has no solid determination of its meaning.

In what year did Pele first play a game in the U.S.?
By the time he signed with the New York Cosmos in 1975,
Pele had been to the U.S. a number of times. The first time
he played here was in 1966. Santos, his club team, played
Portugal's Benfica in August at Downing Stadium. In
September Santos returned to play Inter Milan in Yankee
Stadium. During a 1968 trip, Santos played the New York
Generals and won 5-3. Pele played in that game but was
held scoreless while being marked by Gordon Bradley.
When Pele joined the Cosmos a couple years later, Bradley
was Pele's coach.

Did Pele invent the bicycle kick?
In a Pele biography by Harry Harris, Pele tells of learning
the bicycle kick from one of his youth coaches. That coach,
Valdemar de Brito, had played for Brazil during the 1934
World Cup along with Leonidas. Pele attributes the bicycle
kick to Leonidas.

**What happened to Angelo Anastasio when the New
York Cosmos signed Pele?**
Before the New York Cosmos signed Pele, the team had a
full roster. Anastasio had joined the Cosmos the prior year
but was released to make room for the Brazilian. He never
again played in the NASL.

How many seasons did Pele play in the NASL?
His legacy included providing legitimacy for the league,
luring other world stars to the U.S., and kick-starting the
game among millions of American kids. However, his
actual time here was less than three seasons. He arrived
during the middle of the 1975 season and played through
the 1977 season.

Did Pele play in the 1970 World Cup?
After being assaulted in the 1966 World Cup and

announcing that he would not return to the tournament
again, Pele changed his mind. He did play. And he led his
team to another championship, Brazil's third. The exposure
made him one of the most recognizable people on the
planet, giving him fame even in the United States.

**While playing in the NASL, how many seasons did Pele
lead the league in goal scoring?**
He came into the league mid-season in 1975 and scored
five goals. In 1976 Pele scored 13, and scored the same
number in 1977. None of those totals was good enough for
the scoring title. By comparison Steve David, of Miami,
led the league with 23 in 1976. Even though Giorgio
Chinaglia joined the Cosmos after the 1977 season had
begun, he scored twice in his first game and ended the
season leading the league with 19 goals. Steve David,
having moved to Los Angeles, led the league with 26 in
1977.

**What other NASL team was trying to lure Pele to play
for them?**
In the NASL, competition to sign players was as fierce as
competition to win games. Unlike the MLS, recruiting
players was done without league coordination. That was
quite apparent when Lamar Hunt's team, the Dallas
Tornado, went after Pele. Hunt met with Pele in Frankfurt,
Germany. There, Pele told Hunt that Clive Toye, of the
Cosmos, was already pitching the idea of playing in the
U.S.

**After Pele joined the New York Cosmos, which was the
first team that he played against in the NASL?**
The game was a metaphor for the league's struggle of
foreign-versus-domestic players. The Cosmos, led by Pele,
met the Dallas Tornado, captained by American golden boy

Kyle Rote Jr., in Dallas in front of 78,700 fans. With the Tornado up 2-1, Pele scored to tie the game, where it ended.

How many club teams did Pele play on?

Even though South American soccer players typically were exported to Europe in exchange for needed money to keep South American clubs operating, Pele was forced to stay with Santos, the team he joined at 16 years old. While he was still in his teens and European clubs' offers were escalating, the Brazil government declared him a non-exportable national treasure, forcing him to stay in Brazil. After retiring from the game and taking some time off, he joined the New York Cosmos, his second and last club team.

What did Pele accomplish in his last NASL match?

He won an NASL championship against the Seattle Sounders. It was not his final game, however. That came after the Cosmos made some money off him with a world tour. Then the team returned to New York, where the Cosmos took on Santos for Pele's final game.

In his farewell game, how many goals did Pele score?

Playing half the game for his U.S. team, the Cosmos, and the other half for his only other club team, Santos, Pele managed some good touches on the ball but no goals. In fact, he did not have an assist either.

A former MLS player, Curt Onalfo's birthday was a bench-mark day for Pele. What did Pele do on the day Onalfo was born?

Onalfo became an assistant coach with the U.S. Men's National Team. Before that he played in MLS with L.A., San Jose, and D.C. Before that, on November 19, 1969, he was born. On that same day Pele scored his 1000th goal.

Goals

During the 20th Century two goals scored by U.S. men were labeled "The Shot Heard 'Round the World". Which goals were they?

Schoolhouse Rock, those Saturday morning mini-cartoons aimed at educating children who watched television instead of read books, had one episode about The Shot Heard 'Round the World. That episode explained that the phrase was a reference to the musket shot that began the Revolutionary War, the series of battles that earned the American colonies independence from mighty England. When the two nations met in the 1950 World Cup, one shot—this one from a forward's head—again led to a remarkably successful underdog effort. The U.S. won 1-0 in the biggest upset in the history of the World Cup. Due to the similarities, the 1950 header that scored the game's lone goal became known as The Shot Heard 'Round the World. For 39 years that goal was the U.S.'s greatest highlight on the world stage of soccer. We changed that on November 19, 1989, when the U.S. earned a trip back to the World Cup with another stunning shot which led to another 1-0 upset. Playing Trinidad and Tobago away in the final game of qualifying for the 1990 World Cup, the U.S. team brought home a victory by way of a Paul Caligiuri shot from 35 yards out. The phrase was then applied to Caligiuri's goal. This later event deserves the title more, wrote soccer historian David Litterer, even though the rest of the world knows better the 1950 upset. "[The victory over Trinidad and Tobago] showed the world that the Americans were doormats no longer."

Who scored the golden goal in overtime that gave D.C. United the victory in MLS Cup '96?

The first MLS game was a little disappointing for television viewers, but the championship game of that year was spill -

your-beer exciting. The Los Angeles Galaxy led the game 2-0 in the second half at Foxboro Stadium. Rain was as plentiful as noise. D.C. United tied the score and forced extra time. Then came Eddie Pope, a member of the U.S. Olympic team that year while still finishing classes at the University of North Carolina. His life had been so crazy that when National Team Coach Steve Sampson asked him to come into the national team camp, Pope said that he was too busy. Then came a ball from a Marco Etcheverry corner kick and Pope headed it past Jorge Campos into the Galaxy net to win the 1996 crown for D.C. Sampson again asked Pope to come into national team camp. This time he accepted and ended up playing for the U.S. for 11 years.

Through 2005, who is the only player to score in consecutive MLS championship games?
With his team down 2-0 in MLS Cup '96, Tony Sanneh started the comeback with a goal that led D.C. United to an overtime victory. In MLS Cup '97 Sanneh scored D.C.'s second, and deciding, goal.

Who scored the lone goal in the 1950 World Cup match between the U.S. and England?
Walter Bahr took a shot that, he said for years, likely would have been saved by Bert Williams, England's goalkeeper. However, Joe Gaetjens dove toward the ball and redirected it with his head, sending it into the net.

How many more games did Joe Gaetjens play for the U.S. after the 1950 World Cup?
Gaetjens had not appeared in any of the qualifiers prior to the 1950 World Cup. And after the tournament he never again played for the U.S. Men's National Team. Instead of becoming a U.S. citizen, as he previously had stated that he would, he returned to Haiti. There he joined Haiti's national team (something no longer allowed by FIFA rules)

and played in qualifying games against Mexico for the 1954
World Cup. Sadly, Gaetjens dropped out of sight years later
and was believed to be the victim of a political murder.

How many goals did the United States Women's National Team score in the qualifying tournament for the 1991 Women's World Cup?

The United States Women's National Team qualified as the
one team from CONCACAF by beating five other teams
with a composite score of 49-0. The U.S. continued to
dominate when the team reached China for the Women's
World Cup, scoring 25 more goals while giving up 5.

Who leads the U.S. Women's National Team in total goals scored?

Having scored against 31 different national teams, Mia
Hamm racked up 158 international goals before retiring in
2004. With such a strong reputation, Hamm never was able
to win a goal-scoring title in the World Cup or the
Olympics. In fact she only scored eight World Cup goals
and five Olympic goals. During those times when she drew
multiple defenders, Hamm dished out assists, ending her
career with 114 of them.

Has anybody ever scored goals in his first five games with the U.S. Men's National Team?

Eddie Johnson's run of scoring in each of his first four U.S.
Men's National Team appearances is a record. And it's
even more impressive considering that all four games were
World Cup qualifiers. After those four matches, the U.S.
took on Columbia in a friendly. Johnson was in the line-up,
but he failed to keep the string alive.

When the U.S. played Columbia in the 1994 World Cup, what U.S. player scored?

The first U.S. goal was scored when a Columbian defender

misdirected a pass into his team's goal. The second goal, a far more conventional one, started with Marcelo Balboa winning a ball in the U.S. penalty area, dribbling it out, and passing toward his near touchline. It came back to Balboa with a one-touch pass, and he then one-touched it up the field by 10 yards to a teammate. The U.S. then played it wide, followed by another one-touch pass into the center of the field. We passed it toward the half-way line, dribbled the ball back, and sent it wide to the other side of the field. There, John Harkes took two touches toward the inside and chipped a 15-yard ball past four Columbia defenders. Earnie Stewart met it first time to knock it past the goalkeeper and off the near post to end the full-field play that involved a total of 18 touches, 8 of them passes. Stewart then ran into a celebration that was goofier than Sylvester Stallone's penalty-saving jig from the movie *Victory*. Commentator Seamus Malin compared the second goal to the first goal by saying, "Nothing tainted about this one."

During the 2002 World Cup, how many minutes were needed for the U.S. to equal the total goals it scored in the 1998 World Cup?

In 1998 the U.S. scored one goal in the World Cup. In 2002 the U.S. played its first game against Portugal, one of the favorites to win the tournament. With an offensive mind-set, the Americans scored during the fourth minute after a corner kick. We scored two more within 36 minutes. However, there was an uncomfortable similarity about that game: in the 1966 World Cup Portugal had gone down quickly 3-0 to underdog North Korea only to battle back to win 5-3. In this 2002 match, though, the best the European team could muster was two goals, allowing us a 3-2 victory.

Who is the only U.S. male to score in more than one World Cup?

Even though the U.S. played in back-to-back World Cups in 1930 and 1934 and has made every tournament since 1990, only one person has scored in multiple versions. The goal scorers of 1990, were Paul Caligiuri and Bruce Murray. The goal scorers of 1994 were Eric Wynalda and Earnie Stewart. Only Brian McBride scored in France in 1998. McBride then scored in Asia in 2002 against Portugal and Mexico. Landon Donovan also scored in 2002 (twice), as did Clint Mathis (against South Korea) and John O'Brien. Clint Dempsey scored for the U.S. in 2006.

Among the alterations of indoor soccer is the size of the goals. What was the height of MISL goals based on?
The NASL played indoor tournaments with goals that measured 4 feet high by 16 feet wide. MISL commissioner Earl Foreman, league organizer Ed Tepper, and others met prior to the first MISL season to alter rules for a more exciting game. Tepper walked to a door where the MISL group was meeting and gave his thoughts: the goals for indoor soccer should be as tall as the door frame. The rest agreed.

Who scored 19 goals in 18 games leading up to the 1992 Olympics but was left out of the U.S.'s opening match of the Olympics?
Feeling that the U.S. needed more speed up front than Steve Snow had to offer, Coach Lothar Osiander left him out of the team's 2-1 loss to Italy. Snow came back to score two goals in the next two games, but the U.S. left the tournament without advancing.

How many goals did Mo Johnston score in his first game with Kansas City?
That game on May 2, 1996, became legendary. Johnston had landed in Kansas City from Scotland two days earlier, started that game, and helped set up his team's first goal

just five minutes in. Brian McBride, of the Columbus
Crew tied it in the 20th minute, and both teams went into
halftime. Two minutes after the break, Johnston scored.
Kansas City 2-1. Then the Crew's Todd Yeagley scored, the
Crew's Mike Clark scored, and a Kansas City defender
knocked one into his own net. Crew 4-2 with 24 minutes
left. Preki, chipped a PK into the middle of the goal for
K.C, and then Johnston scored again—his second. Tie
game at 4. Mike Sorber scored for K.C., and then Preki
netted another to end the game 6-4.

**Even though he gave up five goals in the 1997 MLS all-
star game and was on the loosing side by a score of 5-4,
goalie Jorge Campos had something to smile about after
that game. What?**
Compos came into the game in the first half for the West
all-stars. He came in as a forward and scored his team's
second goal for a 2-0 lead. During the second half he
played goalie, where he gave up a handful of goals. The
goal he scored was his first in MLS During the next season
Campos was traded to Chicago, where he assisted twice as
a field player and assisted twice as a goalkeeper.

Penalty Kicks

**On June 2004 Jose Cancela scored a penalty kick for his
team, the New England Revolution, but ended up
apologizing to his teammates after the game. Why?**
Cancela took a PK in the 62nd minute by chipping an easy
ball down the middle of the goal. Columbus goalkeeper,
Jon Busch, expecting something mightier, picked a side
only to watch the ball float over the line where he had been
standing. Later in the game, with New England down 2-1
in injury time, the team was awarded another PK. Cancela
took the PK and again chipped down the middle. Busch

stood firm and let the ball land in his arms. Cancela said later that he was surprised that Busch "would think I was going to shoot the same way."

Brandi Chastain missed a penalty kick in a game months prior to the 1999 World Cup final. Which team was that PK against?
Prior to her renowned shot that ended the 1999 World Cup, Chastain actually had missed two important PKs in her career. The first was during the NCAA semifinals in 1990, when she missed one for her Santa Clara team, allowing Connecticut to advance to the championship match. Nine years later, and four months prior to shucking her jersey, she took a PK against China and the same 'keeper she would later face in the World Cup championship game. Chastain missed and later said China's goalkeeper upset her confidence by making eye contact. As she strode toward the penalty spot at the end of the 1999 World Cup final, Chastain avoided eye contact with the Chinese goalie and converted the winner.

Against South Korea in the 2002 World Cup, the United States gave up a penalty kick. Who committed the foul?
Jeff Agoos committed the foul and earned a yellow card. Agoos, who had played in every qualifier to get the U.S. into the World Cup, had a disastrous tournament. After the 2002 World Cup, he gave up playing for the U.S., cut his hair, and dominated at defense in Major League Soccer.

What was the result of that penalty kick?
With the U.S. ahead 1-0, Lee Eul Yong took the kick but saw it blocked by Brad Friedel. Friedel continued to shine in that game as the South Koreans out-shot the U.S. 19-6. South Korea did score one to earn a draw.

According to U.S. National Team Coach Bruce Arena, what nation has the best method for taking penalty kicks?

Long before he was coaching the U.S. Men's National Team, Arena was the coach of the University of Virginia and doing a pretty good job of it. Just prior to the beginning of the 1985-86 season, Arena was working with his players and decided to show them the best way to take penalty kicks. He said the German Bundesliga had the right approach—rip a shot as hard as possible. He then demonstrated by shooting, turning around to his players, and passing out. His trainers eventually decided that Arena, in emphasizing his commitment to the German style of PKs had pulled his quad muscle and fainted from the pain.

Since 1990 the United States Men's National Team has faced six penalty kicks in the World Cup. How many have been scored?

Playing in Italy in 1990, Italy got a PK but hit the post. Czechoslovakia was awarded two that same year, but scored only one. In 2002 Brad Friedel faced two PKs, one versus Poland, one versus South Korea. He saved the one against Poland, but the U.S. still lost 3-1. He also saved the one against South Korea, allowing the U.S. to finish the game 1-1. The concocted PK against Ghana in 2006 reached the net, only the second of the six to go in.

When Landon Donovan scored in the 2001 MLS All-star game, what did he mock with his celebration?

Reminding people of Brandi Chastain's triumphant penalty kick that ended the 1999 Women's World Cup, Donovan shucked his jersey and revealed a woman's sports bra.

Awards and Honors

During the first 10 seasons of MLS, only one person has won MVP honors twice. Who?
He first won it in 1997, when he led the league in goals. In 2003 Preki again scored more goals than any other player and was one of only eight players in the league to play all 30 of a team's regular season games. Three days before his 40th birthday, on Preki Bobblehead Night, he scored one goal and provided three assists. Throughout the entire 2003 season he either scored or assisted on 29 of the team's 48 goals. For that effort, he again was named MVP.

Who was the only six-time MVP of the MISL?
Known as the king of indoor soccer, Steve Zungul won MVP in the MISL in 1979, 1980, 1981, 1982, 1985, and 1986. He is the league's all-time leader in goals, having scored 652 in 423 games, and was the highest paid soccer player in the country for much of the 1980s. Meanwhile, he won the last MVP award of the outdoor NASL, scoring 20 goals in 24 games for Golden Bay in 1984.

Other than Steve Zungul, who else has won MVP honors in both the MISL and in a U.S. outdoor league?
This guy is a testament to longevity. He was named MVP of the Major Indoor Soccer League in 1989 and MVP of the Continental Indoor Soccer League in 1995. During the 1996 Major League Soccer season, Preki played every minute of every regular season game and playoff game for Kansas City. In 1997 he led the league in scoring and was named league MVP. Noted above, he won that honor again six years later.

During the 1994 World Cup game between Columbia and the U.S., two players were on the field who would later win MLS MVP honors. Who were they?
Tony Meola, who talked about becoming an actor after the 1994 World Cup, was named MVP in 2000 with Kansas City. Columbian Carlos Valderrama won the award in 1996 with Tampa Bay.

What later MLS MVP earned an ejection in the opening game of the 1994 World Cup?
When Bolivia met Germany in the 1994 World Cup opening game, Marco Etcheverry was on the bench for Bolivia. He had not played a game since the previous October due to a knee injury. With his team down 1-0, Etcheverry entered the game in the 79th minute. He was ejected three minutes later. Two years after that, he appeared in the United States again, playing for D.C. United during the first season of MLS. Still prone to outbursts, Etcheverry almost was traded by Coach Bruce Arena. Kept on the team, he led United to three league championships—being named league MVP in 1998—with his stunning accuracy on free kicks, passes, and shots.

What Poland National Team player won most valuable player honors in MLS Cup '98?
In 1998 the Chicago Fire had three Polish stand-outs, including Peter Nowak, a former captain of the Poland National Team. In MLS Cup '98 he assisted on two goals, leading his team to a 2-0 victory and earning him MVP honors.

Who won the MLS Goal of the Year in 2000?
Playing for the Colorado Rapids against the Columbus Crew on April 22, Marcelo Balboa took a cross from about 15 yards out with his back to the goal. He ripped a bicycle

kick into the net and earned goal of the year honors for the
season.

Who was named FIFA Women's World Player of the Year for 2001 and 2002?

The honor was new in 2001. Mia Hamm won it then and
repeated in 2002. For the following year, she finished
second in voting. Prior to that award, Hamm was named
U.S. Soccer's Female Athlete of the Year in 1994, 1995,
1996, 1997, and 1998. She is the only five-time winner.

What is the name of college soccer's award that is equivalent to college football's Heisman Trophy?

Believe it or not there used to be two. First came the
Hermann trophy, named for and awarded by Bob Hermann,
the president of the National Professional Soccer League,
one of the leagues that became part of the North American
Soccer League. Hermann began honoring college soccer's
best player in 1967 and added a woman's award in 1988. In
1986 the Missouri Athletic Club decided to honor the best
soccer player in the country. It added an award for women
in 1991. The two efforts joined together for 2002,
recognizing the top male and female soccer players in
Division I with the M.A.C. Hermann Trophies. The winner
is announced at the Missouri Athletic Club's annual
banquet.

Through the 2005 winners, how many people have won more than one M.A.C. Hermann Trophy?

When Portland's Christine Sinclair won it after the 2005
season, she became the only person to win a second M.A.C.
Hermann Trophy. Prior to 2002, when the two awards
became one, six people won the Hermann Trophy twice. Al
Trost won in 1969 and 1970, and Mike Seery did in 1971
and 1972. Both of them played for St. Louis University.
Playing for Indiana University, Ken Snow won the

Hermann Trophy in 1988 and 1990. Mike Fisher went back to back in 1995 and 1996 with Virginia. Among women Hermann Trophy winners, Mia Hamm did it twice, 1992 and 1993, as did Cindy Parlow. Parlow and Hamm won the M.A.C. awards those same years as well. Among M.A.C. winners, only Claudio Reyna and Ken Snow won two each. Reyna, with Virginia, did it in 1992 and 1993. Snow won the M.A.C. awards of 1988 and 1990.

Porfirio Armando Betancourt played for the Honduras National Team during its three games in the 1982 World Cup. His college credits him as the school's first "to compete for the World Cup". What U.S. college did he attend?
Betancourt, known by his middle name in college and his first name during the World Cup, scored 27 goals for Indiana University and had a total of 63 points in 1981 on his way to winning the Hermann Trophy. He played in all three of Honduras's World Cup games in Spain.

After Mike Fisher was named the best male college soccer player in 1996, what did he go on to do?
Fisher did not go to Disneyland. He did not go into Major League Soccer either. He went to medical school. He was a great American hope after being named the country's best male college soccer player in 1995 and 1996. Even though Fisher had made his intentions known, the Tampa Bay Mutiny used its 1997 first draft pick on Fisher. He kept his word and went to medical school.

Championships

What is the longest running sporting tournament in the United States?
It's the single-elimination tournament to crown the best

soccer team. Open to professional and amateur clubs that register with the United States Soccer Federation, it's a months' long knock-out tournament. Imagine the Major League Baseball playoffs being played during the season and including every minor league and amateur team. Since it's an open tournament, not an invitational one, it has often been known as the U.S. Open Cup. Originally the tournament was called the National Challenge Cup, being sought by teams in the Northeast starting in 1914. The winners received the Dewar Trophy, a gift from Thomas Dewar, a British distiller. The members of the professional North American Foot Ball League dominated the tournament early on. The first winner was the Brooklyn Field Club, a NAFBL team. Bethlehem Steel, also part of the NAFBL, won four of the next five tournaments.

What city was the home of the first national champion of soccer in the United States?
Before the National Challenge Cup and before standard leagues began in the U.S., teams would challenge other teams to something similar to pick-up games. As the teams became more formal, a system similar to boxing's challenges with belts developed. Often two soccer teams would play for a trophy or cup. After citywide leagues began, challenge matches expanded between top teams of different cities with the winner earning bragging rights as being the best in a whole state or region. That led to leagues with wider geographic bases, such as the American Football Association, which formed in 1884. Its first championship was earned in 1885 by ONT, of Kearny, New Jersey. As winners, ONT took home the first American Cup trophy. During the first years of the league, competition was very much limited to communities along the Hudson River, but additional teams made the quest for the American Cup more legitimate as a national championship. After stalling in 1898 and restarting later, the competition for the

American Cup went the way of college basketball's post-season National Invitation Tournament as teams concentrated more on the National Challenge Cup.

What Massachusetts team played as the U.S. Men's National Team in 1947?

In the late 1800's the harbor area of Fall River was converting to an industrial economy with water-powered mills. Its access to the Atlantic helped the area's businesses import and export goods and made it inviting to immigrants from Europe. Those immigrants, most from England and Ireland, brought an interest in soccer with them, and industrial work provided more free time compared to farming. The Bristol County League was formed in 1886 to be followed a year later by the New England Football League. Teams from the area consistently did well in national competitions through the following decades, including a 1947 victory for Ponta Delgada in the U.S. Open Cup, the tournament considered as the championship for all teams in the United States. That team then played as the U.S. National Team for the North American Championship.

How many teams won the U.S. Open Cup in the same year that it won the U.S. Amateur Cup?

The U.S. Soccer Federation has run a tournament specifically for amateur tams, the National Amateur Cup, since 1924. Three times the champion of that tournament has managed to win the U.S. Open Cup during the same year. In 1947 Ponta Delgada, of Fall River, Massachusetts, won both tournaments. The German-Hungary team of New York did it in 1951. Kutis Soccer Club, of St. Louis, was the last one to win both, in 1957.

What team has won the most consecutive National Amateur Championships?

Tom Kutis, president of the Kutis Mortuary in St. Louis, was asked to sponsor a young soccer team but was reluctant because of the injuries supposedly involved in the game. He was coaxed into believing that the stories were exaggerated, getting him to contribute sponsorship money. Attending a game a few weeks later, he witnessed a player break his leg. Nevertheless, Kutis continued and expanded his sponsorship to involve a men's team that included Harry Keogh, one of the members of the 1950 World Cup team. That team won six National Amateur Championships in a row, starting in 1956.

After the Scullins Steel Company of St. Louis and a team from Patterson, New Jersey, tied 2-2 in the final of the National Challenge Cup of 1923, they were told to replay the game in New Jersey. What annual sporting event caused the Scullins team to forfeit?
This was during a time when few people went to college and most people made a living by sweaty, hard work. Also, with no television and few cars, sports was a way to pass the time: People did not quit participating in amateur games when their school years ended, and they were delighted to get the opportunity to make some money at the game. Being a pro athlete usually meant that a guy took home a portion of the admission fees but still worked in a factory or on a farm the next day. Men were quite willing to adapt their skills to multiple sports. Instead of vying for the national championship of soccer, four Scullins players headed off to baseball's spring training, causing the rest of the team to forfeit.

What team has won the U.S. Open Cup the most times?
Bethlehem Steel won its fifth in 1926. The Fall River Marksmen won four and then one more after becoming the New Bedford Whalers. The only other team to win five

was Los Angeles' Maccabee Soccer Club, completing that feat in 1981.

What are the most U.S. Open Cup championship teams that one person has played on?

By the time American players were making names for themselves by playing in Europe at the end of the 20th Century, most people had long forgotten about Billy Gonsalves. For decades he was considered the best American-born soccer player. With Fall River, Massachusetts, he won national titles in 1930 and 1931. He continued his string by winning four more consecutive titles: in 1932 with the New Bedford Whalers, of Massachusetts; in 1933 and 1934 with St. Louis's Stix, Baer & Fuller; and in 1935 with St. Louis's Central Breweries. Gonsalves' teams of 1943 and 1944, Brooklyn Hispano, also won. The next three players who follow Gonsalves on that all-time list played with Gonsalves on several title winners. Of Bill McPherson's seven titles, five were shared with Gonsalves. Alex McNab shared the title with Gonsalves six times, as did Werner Nilsen.

Prior to 2007 who was the last non-MLS team to win the U.S. Open Cup?

Since Major League Soccer began in 1996 as the country's top league, only one team from outside has won the U.S. Open Cup. In 1999 it went to the Rochester Raging Rhinos, of New York. At the time, the team was part of the A-league, one step below MLS. Rochester beat the defending cup champion Chicago Fire in the final. Before that the Rhinos beat three other MLS teams—Dallas, Columbus, and Colorado. The club's success has regularly drawn crowds above 10,000 and encouraged the team to open a new stadium priot to the 2006 season.

What team won the first ever MLS championship?

Long before D.C. United won MLS Cup 96, its first season looked bleak. The team lost the very first MLS game, followed by a 4-0 loss to Columbus. Then it was a 2-1 loss to L.A., 2-1 loss to New England, 3-1 loss to L.A., and 2-1 loss to New York/New Jersey. In the team's seventh game it beat Columbus 5-2 and managed to end the season with 16 wins and 16 losses, good enough to make the playoffs. D.C. lost its first playoff game but won everything from then on.

What team has won the most MLS championships?
The team lost the very first Major League Soccer game and seven of its next nine. D.C. United then turned things around for an incredible run through the season and into the playoffs, where United met the L.A. Galaxy in MLS Cup 96. There, D.C. found themselves down 2-0 but tied the game to win it in overtime. D.C. United won the cup again in 1997, 1999, and 2004, giving the team four championships, the most of MLS.

Through 2006 which teams have lost the most MLS championship games?
After starting the first season of Major League Soccer with a run of 12 straight wins, the L.A. Galaxy reached MLS Cup '96 only to blow a 2-0 lead to D.C. United. The Galaxy also lost in the championship games of 1999 (again to United) and 2001 (to San Jose). In the team's fourth trip to the championship game, it beat the New England Revolution in 2002. New England has lost two other finals, in '05 and '06, to tie L.A. with three second place seasons.

Has D.C. United ever lost an MLS championship game?
After winning MLS Cup 96 and MLS Cup 97, D.C. United scored more goals and won more games in 1998 than it had in either 1996 or 1997. Making its way to the final game, D.C. found itself facing the Chicago Fire, a first-year team.

The match-up appeared to be a David-versus-Goliath show-down, with further similarities in the coaches: Fire Coach Bob Bradley had been the assistant coach for Bruce Arena at D.C. the two previous years. Bradley also had been Arena's assistant at the University of Virginia. Even when Chicago's Jerzy Podbrozny scored in the 29th minute, the Fire was unsettled. During the two previous meetings between the two teams, Chicago had scored first but lost both games by a total score of 7-2. Then Chicago's Diego Gutierrez scored just prior to halftime. With marking by Chris Armas, saves by Zach Thorton, defense by every Fire player, and fouls left and right, Chicago held on for a 2-0 win over D.C.

How far into MLS Cup 96 was the L.A. Galaxy ahead?
L.A. was ahead 2-0 against D.C. United, a team that had not come back from a two-goal deficit all season. D.C.'s Tony Sanneh scored in the 73rd minute, and then Shawn Medved tied the game in the 81st. In overtime D.C. won it.

Which MLS team has been the most successful on the field?
In addition to being the champions of MLS in 1996, 1997, 1999, and 2004, this team was the 1996 U.S. Open Cup winner. The team is D.C. United. It also competed against the best teams in North America, Central America, and the Caribbean in 1998 and won the CONCACAF Champion's Cup. That victory earned D.C. the opportunity to play the best club from South America, for the 1998 Interamerican Cup. D.C. won again, earning the informal title of champions of the Western Hemisphere.

What player has scored goals that clinched three championships for his MLS team?
With the score tied at two in MLS Cup '96, Eddie Pope headed in a corner kick to claim the trophy for D.C. United.

United then went on to play in the club championship of
North America, Central America, and the Caribbean in the
CONCACAF Champion's Cup. In the final of that
tournament, Pope's 41st minute tally proved to be the only
goal of the match, defeating Mexican champion CD Toluca
at RFK Stadium. By winning that match, D.C. United went
on to face the club champion of South America, Brazilian
side CR Vasco da Gama, in the Interamerican Cup. United
slipped at home, losing the home leg of the tourney 1-0.
But three weeks later, United showed its championship
savvy, as Tony Sanneh's first-half goal put United ahead 1-
0. In the 77th minute Pope scored the Cup-winning goal,
giving the team a 2-1 aggregate victory.

**One other MLS team has won the CONCACAF
Champion's Cup. Which one?**
By reaching MLS Cup 1999, the L.A. Galaxy earned a
berth into the 2000 CONCACAF Champion's Cup and
eventually reached the championship match in early 2001.
L.A. had to go penalty kicks to beat Real CD Espana, of
Honduras, in the quarterfinals and then had to go to penalty
kicks in the semifinals to beat D.C. United, the team that
had beaten them in MLS Cup 1999. L.A. met CD Olimpia,
of Honduras, in the final, winning 3-2.

What team won MLS Cup '03?
I'm not going to ask who won each and every MLS
championship game because some were not that
memorable. MLS Cup '03 should stand out because of
how the San Jose Earthquakes got there and won it. First
came a two-game, playoff series that counted total goals.
After losing the opening game 2-0, the Earthquakes found
themselves behind 2-0 to the Los Angeles Galaxy during
the first half of the second game. Several factors made a
comeback from an aggregate score of 4-0 seem impossible:
San Jose's previous four goals against the Galaxy had taken

820 minutes while there were only 70 minutes left in this game; Galaxy goalkeeper Kevin Hartman had never allowed more than two goals in his 37 previous starts; and Hartman had entered the match building a post-season shutout streak of 401 minutes.

Jeff Agoos started the comeback with a goal in the 21st minute. Then came a goal from Landon Donovan, and the teams headed in for halftime. At that point the Earthquakes needed to prevent any goals by the Galaxy and score two more goals just to force overtime. Jamil Walker scored for the Earthquakes soon after half for an aggregate 4-3 score, but then the Galaxy regrouped, holding their own on defense and pressuring San Jose's goal. San Jose Coach Frank Yallop subbed in Rodrigo Faria, and with two minutes left in the game he sent on Chris Roner. Roner scored just before the final whistle, locking the aggregate score at 4-4, sending the series into overtime. There, Faria, without a goal in 723 minutes of play, put in the golden goal that sent San Jose into the conference final.

Facing Kansas City in the one-game conference final, the Earthquakes fell behind in the 57th minute but tied it four minutes later. After allowing another goal, the Earthquakes faced the possibility of heading home until they scored with under seven minutes left. Going into extra time, neither team scored in the first period. In the 117th minute, Landon Donovan won it for the earthquakes, sending the team into MLS Cup '03. In the final San Jose scored two in the first half and held on to win 4-2.

Which MLS team made the playoffs all 10 of the league's first 10 years?
It's the L.A. Galaxy.

Of all the championships in Major League Soccer and the North American Soccer League, how many have

been won by a team during that team's first year in the league?
The Chicago Fire did it with a 2-0 win over D.C. United in MLS Cup 1998. Twenty-five years earlier, the Philadelphia Atoms won the championship of the NASL during its first season in the league. Using a team made primarily of Americans, the Atoms beat Dallas in the title game by the same score, 2-0. In addition to those two times that a first-year team has won a league championship, we cannot forget two other teams: D.C. United, which won MLS's very first title, and the Atlanta Chiefs, which won the NASL's first crown.

When was the first national championship for college soccer played?
The first college soccer games were played on the East Coast and in St. Louis. Gradually schools in the mid-west put together teams. Then came West Coast schools. The first championship that was anything more than regional was the Missouri Soccer Commission's Soccer Bowl, first played on January 1, 1950, as a match between the unbeaten teams from the University of San Francisco and Pennsylvania State University. The game was played in St. Louis, and the teams tied. When Pennsylvania State University met Perdue a year later, the Pennsylvanians won 3-1. Poor weather caused problems for a third game, leaving it to be played in San Francisco in February. The NCAA did not take up soccer until 1959.

When was the first national championship for women's college soccer played?
In 1971 the Association of Intercollegiate Athletics for Women was founded. Nine years later that body organized the first national championship for women's college soccer, which was won by Cortland State College. In 1981 the University of North Carolina won it. NCAA started

crowning a women's champion a year later. The NAIA
(National Association of Intercollegiate Athletics) started a
national soccer tournament for women in 1984. The
National Junior College Athletic Association crowned its
first women's soccer champion in 1982.

Which team won the 1967 National Professional Soccer League title?

When the New York Generals and the Baltimore Bays
played late in the season, New York earned a PK, giving
them the chance to break a tie and stay in the hunt for a
playoff spot. New York Coach Freddie Goodwin saw his
trusted PK appointee walking away from the kick. Unable
to speak the Argentine player's language, Goodwin subbed
the player who was injured for a West German instructed to
take the kick. The West German failed to score. Later the
Argentine, through an interpreter, explained to Goodwin
that he had walked away from the penalty spot to collect his
thoughts before taking the PK. The game ended in a tie,
knocking New York out of the playoff picture. Baltimore
stayed alive and went into the playoffs, eventually reaching
the championship game. There Baltimore lost to the
Oakland Clippers, giving Oakland the one and only NPSL
title before the league became part of the NASL.

How many NASL championships did the New York Cosmos win with Pele?

Other than winning the 1972 title by beating out seven
other teams, the Cosmos before Pele were miserable. He
helped the team reach an even record in his first few games
in 1975, but then the Cosmos went scoreless for the next
264 minutes and finished the season with a 10-12 record.
After the season, Cosmos management worsened the
situation by adding more nationalities and more languages
for a world tour. The most apparent problem was
communication; next was the difference in styles between

South Americans and Europeans. During league play in
1976, however, the team settled down and was helped by
the addition of 28-year-old Italian national team player
Giorgio Chinaglia. The cosmos went 16-8 in 1976 but lost
in the playoffs. At the expense of using American players,
the Cosmos kept raising the level of play by adding more
international stars to the roster. Those additions also added
media attention to the team and expectations. Pele's
personal trainer told one reporter, "If the Cosmos become
champions, it will change a lot [in the United States]." He
called the Cosmos' effort *a coronation* and predicted the
end of NASL's "era of the 3rd and 4th Division English
Players." In 1977, Pele's last year with the team, the
Cosmos brought in West German national teamer Franz
Beckenbauer and won the league. The trainer's forecast
could not have been more incorrect. Those additional
players did help the Cosmos win but also raised the
expectations of fans. When the famous players left, the
fans stayed home.

How many NASL titles did the New York Cosmos win in all?

After winning titles in 1972 and 1977, New York tried to
prove that it could win post-Pele. In the 1978 playoffs the
Cosmos first defeated Seattle, setting up a two-game
playoff series against the Minnesota Kicks. It became one
of the best playoffs in league history. Minnesota was the
underdog but won the first game in Minnesota 9-2. The
second game went to the Cosmos 4-0 in New York. Then
came a mini-game to break the tie. After a scoreless 30
minutes, the series tie-breaker went into a one-on-one, best-
of-five shootout of the kind where players dribble in toward
the goal. Chico Hamilton immediately scored for
Minnesota. New York failed to equalize. Minnesota
missed its second attempt. New York failed to equalize.
Minnesota missed its third attempt. New York failed to

equalize. Minnesota missed its fourth attempt. New York failed to equalize. Minnesota could have put it out of reach, but missed its fifth attempt. On his team's fifth try to tie the tie-breaker, Brazilian Carlos Alberto lobbed a shot over Tino Lettieri's head into the net. Again the teams were tied. They went to sudden death. Minnesota missed. Franz Beckenbauer scored, giving the series win to the Cosmos. New York then beat Portland and Tampa Bay to become the first back-to-back champions of the NASL. The team won only once more, in 1982, for its fourth NASL title.

Through 2006 how many times has the U.S. won the Women's World Cup?

The United States won the first one in China in 1991 and finished third in 1995. The U.S. won it again in 1999 when the finals were played in the U.S. The 2003 tournament was originally scheduled to be played in China but was moved to the U.S., and the hosts finished third.

With World Cup championships in 1991 and 1999 and Olympic gold medals in 1996 and 2004, the U.S. Women's National Team won four senior world titles in 13 years. How many players have been part of all four of those teams?

Mia Hamm, Kristine Lilly, Julie Foudy, Brandi Chastain, and Joy Biefeld Fawcett were on all four of those teams. But Fawcett went a little further. She gave birth to two kids in between earning those titles. Of those four tournaments, she played every minute of every game in two of them—the 1996 Olympics and the 1999 Women's World Cup.

Of those five women, how many have won an NCAA Division I championship as a player?

Foudy's Stanford teams did not. Nor did Chastain's Santa Clara teams. As a college player at the University of California, Joy Biefeld Fawcett made her way to the NCAA

playoffs three of her four years there. Unfortunately, her
Golden Bears never won the tournament, getting knocked
out by Colorado College in 1986, North Carolina in 1987,
and North Carolina in 1988. By contrast Kristine Lilly and
Mia Hamm did win NCAA titles. Each won four. They
played for North Carolina.

**Did Lilly or Hamm win a title in the Women's United
Soccer Association?**
Lilly played the three WUSA seasons with the Boston
Breakers while Hamm played for the Washington Freedom.
Neither of the two won the league crown in 2001 or 2002,
but in the league's final year, Hamm's Freedom won in
overtime. That crown makes Hamm the only person to
have won two World Cups, two Olympic gold medals, four
NCAA Division I championships, and a WUSA title.

Men's World Cup

How often is the World Cup played?
Since 1930 countries have put together teams of their best
players for the World Cup every four years except for
cancellations in 1942 and 1946. Unlike that first version in
Uruguay, when every interested country was invited, now
the tournament involves several months of qualifying to
reach the World Cup.

**When was the first time that the United States appeared
in a World Cup?**
The first World Cup was played in Uruguay in 1930, and
the United States was there. Of course the full story is that
no qualifying was required. We got there because we
signed up to join the other 12 teams. However, once there,
the U.S. Men's National Team showed its skill by beating
Belgium 3-0 and Paraguay 3-0 before losing to Argentina.

Through 2005 what's the best that the U.S. Men's National Team has finished in a World Cup?
That first World Cup, in 1930, was an anomaly in many ways. Protesting the tournament's location, several European teams skipped the travel to Uruguay. There was no qualifying. Also the tournament had the rare characteristic of seeing the United States in the semifinals. The *New York Times* reported that after two victories the U.S. was "considered . . . the most likely winner of the title." The sources for this handicapping were ambiguous "experts". Perhaps the U.S. would have satisfied those experts had injuries not reduced the States to eight fit men, enabling Argentina to beat the U.S. in the semifinals 6-1.

After 1930 when was the next time that the U.S. appeared in the World Cup?
Unlike the 1930 World Cup, the 1934 version required qualifying. The United States team had to get past Mexico first, a game that was played in Rome days prior to the first game of the tournament. The qualifier was not considered part of the World Cup even though the game pitted the two teams against each other within the tournament atmosphere. The U.S. won 4-2, knocking the Mexicans out of the tournament before they were really even in the tournament.

The 2005 movie *The Game of Their Lives* was told through a narrator. What was that narrator's name?
In the movie the narrator lived into the 21st Century to tell the story of the 1950 World Cup, where the U.S. beat England. The real Dent McSkimming had grown up in St. Louis and learned to play soccer. He joined the St. Louis Dispatch as a reporter in 1922 and covered the game for nearly 40 years for St. Louis newspapers. There at his own expense, McSkimming was the only reporter from the States in Brazil. For years afterward he enjoyed retelling the story of the game, comparing it to the possibility that

students from England's Oxford University could be
formed into a baseball team that could beat the New York
Yankees. Unlike his character in the movie, however,
McSkimming died in 1976.

**Who did the U.S. Men's National Team play in its last
warm-up game before setting off for the 1950 World
Cup, where it beat England?**
It was a team of all-stars on tour from England. England's
national team was warming up with games in Europe,
beating Scotland, Portugal, and Belgium. England's
reserve team also toured Europe. This third-string group of
professionals played in Canada and in the U.S., beating the
U.S. Men's National Team 1-0 in New York. The English
all-stars included Stanley Matthews, who would later be
called up to join England's national team, sending him
directly from New York to Brazil. Matthews had played for
England since 1934 and would play for England versus
Spain in the World Cup. In fact his international career
would not end until 1957, and he was knighted for his
service to the nation. However, Mathews was left out of
the line-up in the World Cup game against the U.S.,
something that England's coach was criticized for.

**Of the 11 U.S. players that faced England in the 1950
World Cup, how many were from St. Louis?**
Many years after the World Cup, various books and
newspapers published in England suggested that the United
States' 1950 team was a collection of immigrants, not a
team of U.S. citizens. In reality, only three were non-
citizens while most were second- or third-generation
citizens. Six members of the team had been born in St.
Louis and five of them were from one St. Louis team,
Simpkins Ford. Of the 11 who played against England, five
of them were living in St. Louis. In fact, three of them—

Frank Borghi, Gino Pariani, and Frank Wallace—lived within 200 yards of each other.

Which FIFA confederation does the U.S. belong to?

Confederations were created to serve a role similar to what the Southeastern Conference and Atlantic Coast Conference are to the NCAA. Most global competitions now require qualifying through the confederations. The NCAA similarity continues to the point that members of one confederation place a great emphasis on beating members of their own confederation but support those rivals when those rivals take on a team from a different confederation. In addition to bragging rights, the winners of cross-confederation games generate evidence that their confederation should be given more designated spots in international competitions. The U.S. belongs to the Confederation of North, Central America and Caribbean Association Football. It's better known as CONCACAF.

How many members of England's 1966 World Cup winning team eventually played in U.S. leagues?

Many U.S. residents saw their first soccer games while England was marching through the 1966 World Cup. When the NASL started up two years later, its teams began competing for good players and recognizable names. The most recognizable players, other than Pele, were those from England's national team. In all, seven of the men from England's World Cup team came to the U.S.: Gordon Banks, Bobby Moore, Ian Callaghan, Alan Ball, Geoff Hurst, Peter Bonetti, and George Eastham. There were three reasons the NASL was attractive to foreign players. First, the NASL was a minor league for stronger leagues around the world. It was similar to what winter league baseball in Central America is for Major League Baseball players. Second, most of the best players who came to the league did so after retirement. Those players were offered

decent money without the stress that accompanied other
leagues. Pele's friend Professor Julio Mazzei once said that
he saw some Cosmos' players performing on the field as if
they were on vacation. These guys were receiving ovations
for just showing up. Third, the NASL became a trendy
place to be for world stars—the venue for pick-up games of
the highest level. It became the vacation spot for the upper
crust of soccer with the freedom to walk unnoticed to the
grocery store. The NASL of 1977, possibly its fulcrum,
was a fad with celebrity allure. It was as much a pro league
in the 1970s as dot-coms were an industry in the 1990s.
Both rode bubbles that eventually burst.

**Which club team was listed most often on the roster of
the U.S. Men's National Team of the 1990 World Cup?**
Without a strong domestic league in the U.S., the national
team's administrators worried about keeping their men in
shape. Letting them play in foreign leagues, though, would
hinder the players' availability for warm-up games prior to
the World Cup. The solution was that the United States
Soccer Federation became the club team for several players,
signing them to full-time contracts. Many of the players
were loaned to other teams for small periods, and some
were still in college.

**What member of the 1994 U.S. Men's National Team
was once suspended by FIFA?**
Leaving Uruguay for a better life that did not include
soccer, Fernando Clavijo arrived in New York City in 1979
with $1,000 in his pocket from his playing days with his
former club. He played some pick-up games in between
jobs until friends hooked him up with the American Soccer
League's New York Apollo. The team gave Clavijo a look
and added him to their roster. Without compensation for
their player, Clavijo's former club notified FIFA, which
sought payment and then banned Clavijo for a year. The

Apollo owner came to the rescue with a $10,000 loan, allowing Clavijo to keep playing. He eventually rose to a six-figure salary with the San Diego Sockers and made the U.S. Men's National Team. He played his last national team game on July 4, 1994.

What was the United States Men's National Team assured of when FIFA decided to play the 1994 World Cup in the United States?

Back then two nations were granted spots in each finals without having to go through qualifying—the defending champion and the host nation. The free ride as host would put the U.S. into the tournament automatically, setting aside a decades-old record of failure in qualifying for the World Cup. The U.S.'s lack of success brought out people who said that the U.S. did not deserve to host the tournament. In the midst of the criticism, the U.S. Men's National Team was trying to qualify for the 1990 World Cup. With the ink still wet on FIFA's press releases to hold the 1994 tournament in the U.S., the U.S. provided fuel to its detractors. In a friendly match against Poland, the U.S. lost 2-0. Back to the qualifying round 11 days later, the U.S. played in Kingston, Jamaica, and achieved a scoreless tie.

What country did the U.S. Men's National Team beat in the 1994 World Cup for the U.S.'s first Men's World Cup victory in 44 years?

Pele actually had picked this nation to win the tournament. It was Columbia, a team that ended up losing another match and heading home with only one victory.

How long had David Regis been a U.S. citizen prior to playing in his first game for the U.S. Men's National Team?

David Regis was born in Martinique, a French territory in the Caribbean, and went on to play in Europe. Just months prior to the 1998 World Cup, he was being scouted by the France National Team. When U.S. Coach Steve Sampson got word that Regis was married to an American woman, Sampson approached him about becoming a U.S. citizen in time to play in that year's World Cup, which just happened to be set in France. He became a citizen on May 17, 1998, and played for the U.S. 29 days later. He played in one more warm-up game and then started all three games during the World Cup. If his contributions to the U.S. team seem unworthy of being selected for the 1998 World Cup, he made up for it afterward. On the road to the 2002 World Cup, Regis played in 12 of 16 qualifiers, the second most of any American for that round.

Among the 32 teams in France in 1998, where did the U.S. finish?
The final game for the U.S. was against Yugoslavia, a 1-0 loss. That put the United States with zero points after three games and with -4 net goals. Japan also finished group play with zero points, but had -3 net goals, leaving the United States last of the 32 teams. However, many soccer haters were proud to say that the United States was the worst team in the world. They forgot or ignored those 142 nations that never qualified for the finals at all.

Which of these national teams went the farthest in the 2002 World Cup—defending champion France, three-time champion Argentina, three-time champion Italy, pre-tournament favorite Portugal, 1998's third-place finisher Croatia, Turkey, or the United States?
France went home after its three first-round games. Argentina did the same. Italy was beaten by South Korea in the round of 16. Portugal, starting the finals with a loss to the U.S., made it no further than three games. Croatia also played only three games. The U.S. went to the

quarterfinals. Turkey lost in the semifinals and won the third place game.

How many positions did Landon Donovan start at during the 2002 World Cup?

In the opener versus Portugal, Donavan played forward. In the next game, versus South Korea, he stepped back to be the right midfielder. Then he played left midfielder against Poland. Against Mexico he played center midfielder, his fourth position, before going back to forward to face Germany.

What three teams did the U.S. play in the first round of the 2002 Men's World Cup?

Our sequence of games was Portugal, South Korea, and Poland. The conventional wisdom predicted that getting into the second round would involve a loss to Portugal, a victory over South Korea, and at least a tie against Poland. None of those results was realized. We beat Portugal, tied South Korea, and lost to Poland—still good enough to get us into the next round.

When the South Koreans scored against the U.S., what Olympic incident was depicted in their post-goal celebration?

South Korea knotted the game at one with 12 minutes remaining. In celebration, most of the team ran to a corner flag and acted as if they were ice skating. The reference was to a situation from the 2002 Winter Olympics, just four months earlier. South Korean short-track speed skater Kim Dong-sung had finished first in the men's 1500-meter race but was disqualified by judges, a decision that gave the gold medal to American Apolo Ohno.

Who knocked the United States out of the 2002 World Cup?

For the 13th consecutive time, Germany made the quarterfinals of a World Cup. The United States was in the quarterfinals for only the second time in its history. When Germany and the U.S. met in the 2002 quarterfinals Germany outscored us, 1-0, even though we led on shots, 11-6, and shots on goal, 6-2. The poetic justice of that game stemmed from the fact that Tony Sanneh had played for F.C. Nuremberg, of the top league in Germany, when the club came to the end of the 2002 season needing a victory to stay in the top league. Their second-to-last week's opponent, Bayer Leverkusen, was on top of the league and needed a victory toward winning the league title. F.C. Nuremberg got the upset, knocking Leverkusen from the top spot and depriving them the championship by one point. Five of the Leverkusen players went on to play for Germany's national team that summer against Sanneh and the U.S. Men's National Team in the World Cup. There, the Germans got revenge on Sanneh by handing him and his teammates a loss.

World Cup Qualifying

Did the U.S. participate in the 1930 World Cup?
In 1930 the U.S. qualified because we agreed to make the trip to Uruguay, where the first World Cup was held. We had to play no qualifiers, nor did the other 12 that participated.

Did the U.S. participate in the 1934 World Cup?
In 1934 we made it to the tournament by winning a one-game qualifier. That qualifier was actually played in Italy, the same location of the tournament, just days before the opening game.

Did the U.S. participate in the 1938 World Cup?

In 1938 the U.S. did not even attempt to qualify for the World Cup. With military and political unrest in Europe, we decided that France was not the place to spend the summer. We ended up visiting France in 1944 instead.

Other than Mexico, which North American country did the U.S. have to play as part of qualifying for the 1950 World Cup?

To get to the 1950 World Cup, the United States had to qualify through the North American Championships in Mexico in 1949. The top two teams among Cuba, Mexico, and the U.S. would go on to the 1950 tournament in Brazil. The U.S. lost twice to Mexico but tied and beat Cuba, earning a spot in the 1950 World Cup with Mexico.

Which country beat out the U.S. to qualify for the 1954 World Cup?

During qualifying for the 1954 World Cup, the U.S. faced Mexico and Haiti each twice, finishing second among the three. With only one spot available, Mexico went to Switzerland for the finals. The U.S. stayed home.

Which North American country played in the 1958 World Cup?

Qualifying for the 1958 finals involved Mexico, Canada, and the U.S. being placed in a preliminary group together. The U.S. lost all four games, and Mexico went ahead to face Costa Rica. Mexico won that series and went on to the finals in Sweden. The U.S. stayed home.

Which North American country played in the 1962 World Cup?

Placed with Mexico in a subgroup again for the 1962 tournament, the U.S. team tied and lost. After those two games, we were out and Mexico was headed on to eventually win a spot in the finals in Chile.

Which North American country played in the 1966 World Cup?

In 1966 Mexico knocked out the U.S. again. The two teams had been set with Honduras, a group in which Mexico gained seven points to the U.S.'s four points in four games. Mexico advanced to the final qualifying round and then to England for the World Cup. The U.S. stayed home.

Which country knocked the U.S. out of qualifying for the 1970 World Cup?

The good news was that Mexico was not competing for the one slot allotted to CONCACAF, the region that includes the U.S. As the host of the tournament, Mexico was given an automatic berth, leaving hope for the United States. Within a group also including Canada and Bermuda, the United States won three and lost one, well enough to earn a place in the next round versus Haiti. At that point, the U.S. lost 2-0 and 1-0. Haiti went on to meet El Salvador, the winner over Honduras, in a series that culminated in the Soccer War of Central America. El Salvador prevailed and went to the World Cup in Mexico.

Did the U.S. participate in the 1974 World Cup?

For 1974 qualifying, the U.S. was placed with Canada and Mexico in a preliminary group. Once again the U.S. failed to move on with three losses and one draw. Mexico went into the next round, but was surprised by Haiti, which advanced to the tournament in Germany.

Which North American country reached the 1978 World Cup?

The preliminary group was the same as it had been in 1974—Mexico, United States, and Canada. However, changes allowed two of the three to advance to the final qualifying group instead of only one. In the fourth game of qualifying, the U.S. beat Canada, inciting the U.S. players to jog a celebratory lap around the Kingdome. With four points to Canada's three and Mexico's three, the U.S. players were sure that they would finish at least second even though Mexico and Canada still had to face each other once more. Banking on Mexico beating Canada, the U.S. players knew that a second place finish meant a berth into the final round of qualifying. When Mexico and Canada played, though, they tied, leaving all three teams with four points. Mexico got first because of goal difference, but the other tie-breakers could not separate the U.S. and Canada for second. The two teams were called on to play off for second place. Canada won 3-0, knocking out the U.S. Mexico ended up winning the next round and headed to the tournament.

Did the U.S. play in the 1982 World Cup?
Qualifying for the 1982 tournament had the U.S. pitted with Canada and Mexico again in the first round. The States won one, lost two, and tied one, allowing Mexico and Canada to move on to the next round. However, neither reached the World Cup. Honduras and El Salvador were the confederation's team that went to Spain.

Which North American countries participated in the 1986 World Cup?
The familiar first-round foes changed. Mexico, as host, did not have to qualify. Placed with Costa Rica and Trinidad and Tobago, the U.S. took off with two wins and a tie—five points. Entering the final game of the group, Costa Rica versus the U.S., Costa Rica needed a win while the U.S. needed a tie to continue. Costa Rica got a 1-0 win. Nevertheless, Costa Rica failed to get past Canada in the next round, allowing our northern neighbors to head to Mexico for the 1986 World Cup. This led to the gray days of American soccer: The NASL had folded; FIFA had chosen Mexico to host the 1986 World Cup over the U.S.'s

bid; and the U.S. failed once again to qualify for the World
Cup. Roger Allaway and Colin Jose wrote in *The United
States Tackles the World Cup*, "Elimination left the future of
American soccer looking very bleak."

Did the U.S. play in the 1990 World Cup?
Even without Mexico competing against the U.S. for a spot
in the 1990 Men's World Cup, the U.S. did not have an easy
time getting through regional qualifying. First, the Yanks
had history against them. In the most previous nine
attempts to reach the World Cup, the U.S. had failed nine
times. Then the U.S. had a slew of competitors who were
willing to fight tooth and nail to reach the tournament.
Qualifying started with a tie in Jamaica. When the
Jamaicans came to the U.S., the Americans won 5-1,
sending the United States into the final round of
CONCACAF qualifying. In that round, the United States
twice would face each opponent (Costa Rica, Trinidad and
Tobago, El Salvador, and Guatemala) with the top two
teams going to Italy. Wins would earn two pints; ties would
earn one. The U.S. lost its first game, in Costa Rica, 1-0.
The return game gave the U.S. two points by way of a 1-0
victory with the help of two Costa Rica goals being called
back and David Vanole saving a penalty kick in the 88th
minute. The next match, a 1-1 tie against Trinidad and
Tobago, earned the U.S. its third point. Playing host again,
the Americans beat Guatemala with an own-goal in June to
reach five points. By mid-July, the U.S. stood alone in
second place with five points behind Costa Rica's 11
points. As positive as the second place status seemed, it
was tempered by the number of games (opportunities to
gain more points) remaining for three teams behind the U.S.
Guatemala had four games to come. Trinidad and Tobago
had five games to play, and El Salvador had the full eight.
Two weeks later Trinidad and Tobago moved within one
point of the U.S. by beating El Salvador. When Trinidad

and Tobago drew against El Salvador in August, the Americans found themselves tied for second and six points away from first. Then T&T moved ahead by defeating Guatemala in August and added two more points by beating Guatemala again in September. When September 17 arrived, the United States had not played a qualifying game in exactly three months and was sitting four points out of second place. The good news was that T&T had one game remaining while the U.S. had four. That September 17 match against El Salvador earned the U.S. two points. But then we went into a skid. The U.S. went scoreless for a tie against Guatemala. When we returned to home soil to play the winless El Salvadorans, we tied 0-0 again, leaving the U.S. in a tie for second place with T&T. All that remained of the schedule was a match-up between T&T and the U.S. in Port of Spain. The islanders celebrated ahead of the game, knowing that a tie with the U.S. would keep T&T ahead on goal difference and net goals, sending them into the World Cup. Paul Caligiuri upset the host's plans, though, finding the net on a 35-yard dipping shot for a 1-0 victory in front of 35,000 red-clad Trinidadians. The win sent the U.S. to the World Cup for the first time since 1950.

How did the U.S. reach the 1994 World Cup?

For most versions of the World Cup, FIFA has given automatic berths to the host nations and the previous cup winners. Being the host in 1994, the United States got into the World Cup without any qualifying games. Germany came as the defending champions. For the 2006 World Cup, FIFA changed the automatic berths to exclude the previous champion. Brazil, the 2002 World Cup winner, had to qualify for the 2006 finals.

Who did the U.S. play in its last game of qualifying for the 1998 World Cup?

The first round of qualifying involved six games. Passing

that test, the U.S. went on to a round of 10 games. By contrast to the 1970s—three near misses in qualifying for the World Cup—the 1998 final round of qualifying games was full of breaks that went the way of the U.S. Against Jamaica in March 1997, Mike Burns cleared a shot off the U.S. goal line to keep the score at 0-0, where the game ended. A month later Mexico gave up an own goal that helped the U.S. tie them 2-2. In the next game, against Jamaica, Eric Wynalda scored the tying goal on a penalty kick for a handball that replays showed occurred outside the penalty area. In the second game against Mexico, a 0-0 tie, Mexico's Luis Garcia reached a ball five yards from the U.S. goal but nodded it wide with just minutes to go. Including the points from those four tie games, the United States placed second in the final group, earning a spot in the 1998 World Cup in France. A ticket to the World Cup was actually assured before the U.S. played its last qualifier. That final game was against El Salvador on November 16, 1997. El Salvador still needed to earn a berth. With the knowledge that the U.S. would be out nothing but pride, somebody placed a call to U.S. players Roy Wegerle and John Harkes, offering money for them to throw the game. The two refused, and the United States won 4-2. El Salvador stayed home.

Who did the U.S. play in its last game of qualifying for the 2002 World Cup?
As was the case in 1998, the U.S. played six games in the semifinal round and 10 in the final round of qualifying. In that final round the U.S. found itself in second place with one game left. Assured of qualifying, we let down in the final game and tied the last place team. The cruelty to that tie was that it came against Trinidad and Tobago, the team that had needed only a tie in the last game of qualifying to go on to the World Cup 12 years earlier.

International Relations

In 1883 the Irish-American Athletic Clubs in the U.S. played soccer games to raise money for Patrick O'Donnell. What did he need the money for?

A man named James Carey had once been a member of a violent organization set on gaining independence for Northern Ireland. While being tried for two murders, Carey turned informer, angering Irishmen all over the world. He later traveled to Africa by ship and was murdered. On that same shape ship was O'Donnell, who was accused of the murder. The money from the soccer games went toward O'Donnell's defense of the charge.

Why did French fans root for our opponents when the United States Olympic Soccer Team faced Estonia in the 1924 Olympic Games in Paris?

First off, they were irritable about the fact that the U.S. had saved their hides just a few years earlier in World War I. Second, they were sure that they would never again need any help from the United States. More likely, however, they cheered for Estonia because the United States rugby team had beaten the French rugby team for the Olympic gold medal the week prior in a huge upset. Al Michaels would have called it a miracle on grass. The jeers of the French notwithstanding, the U.S. beat Estonia in soccer on May 25, 1-0.

When France was defending the World Cup trophy it had won in 1998, how did it do in its opening game of the 2002 World Cup?

To open the tournament, France lost to Senegal 1-0. The anti-Americans pretty much dropped their rifles at that point, mustering a tie and another loss to exit the tournament goal-less in the first round.

How did the United States Soccer Federation (under a former name) raise money to buy soccer equipment for men in the armed forces during World War I?
The United States Football Association, which later became the United Stated Soccer Federation, started a chain letter from its offices in New York, asking each person who received the letter to mail in 25 cents and send a copy of the letter to four other people.

How many individuals appeared for the U.S. Men's National Team in games both before and after World War II?
Too often Americans think of World War II as starting on December 7, 1941. In reality Hitler was waltzing through France and fighting through the rest of Europe much earlier. International soccer was severely curbed during that time. Qualifying for the 1938 World Cup did not include some nations because they had become part of Germany. The U.S. chose to forgo the tournament, being held in Italy, because of unrest on the continent. Then the World Cups of 1942 and 1946 were cancelled. When the war ended, 10 years had passed between games for the U.S. Men's National Team. The U.S.'s first game after World War II, in 1947, was part of the championship of the North American Football Confederation. In that first post-war game, Joseph Michaels appeared, as he had in 1937 against Mexico. Nobody else from the pre-war years ever played for the U.S. team after World War II.

What did Henry Kissinger show President Richard Nixon in September 1970 that nearly caused another Cuban Missile Crisis?
Secretary of State Henry Kissinger met with H.R. Haldeman and President Richard Nixon to review aerial photos of Cienfuegos, Cuba. This was eight years after the Cuban Missile Crisis, which had been resolved when the

Soviet Union agreed to leave the island nation. Kissinger showed photos of soccer fields in Cuba and explained, "Cubans play baseball. Russians play soccer." The photos were the first warning that Soviet men were implementing launching plans in Cuba. Working quietly and without media attention, Nixon and Kissinger convinced the Soviets to stop construction on the Cuban base within two months.

How many times did the U.S. Men's National Team beat the Soviet Union during the Cold War?
If the matches had been for world domination, we would be drinking a lot more vodka right now. The U.S. men and the Soviet men played twice in 1979 and twice in 1990. We lost 4-1, 3-1, and 3-1 before getting a 0-0 draw that must have proven to them the superiority of capitalism.

Who did the U.S. Men beat during the 1992 Olympic soccer tournament in Spain?
We started off with a 2-1 loss to Italy and finished with a 2-2 tie with Poland. In between was a 3-1 win over Kuwait, which came barely a year after the U.S. military had rescued Kuwait from Iraq.

There was an unanswered political question that caused concern just prior to the 1998 World Cup game between the United States and Iran. What was it?
Without diplomatic ties since Iranians took over our embassy and citizens in 1979, the scheduled match drew a lot of attention. Tournament organizers grew even more concerned when Iran team officials refused to commit their team to walk to the U.S. players prior to the game to the shake their hands. As the lower ranked team, Iran was expected to make the gesture. Offering a remedy, the United States players made the short walk to the Iranian side, and the two teams posed for a pre-match photo

together. Typically those photos are taken of the teams separately.

What military event in 1999 created a scare that China would boycott the 1999 Women's World Cup in the United States?
Hardly a month prior to the start of the tournament, American military airplanes mistakenly bombed the Chinese embassy in Belgrade, Yugoslavia. China stayed in the tournament and met the Americans in the final. Leaders of the two countries, Bill Clinton and Deng Xiaoping, used the final to reestablish contact and eventually worked out trade problems.

U.S. Versus Europe and South America

What organization annually hosted top-level foreign teams to the United States for several decades?
The Sodality Football League was formed in 1893 of teams from Catholic organizations in St. Louis to provide cleaner play. What that church-based league also did, quite simply, was give teams stability with a place to store their equipment, hold team meetings, and display trophies. Then the Catholic Church began forming Catholic Youth Councils in 1937 in every U.S. diocese as a means of developing "religious, social, cultural, and physical activities of Catholic youth." With a history of adult soccer via the parishes of St. Louis, the C.Y.C.'s physical activities focused on soccer. As a fund-raiser and get-together for its teams, the C.Y.C. of St. Louis started hosting foreign teams in 1954 to play St. Louis's top clubs, all-star teams, or other foreign teams. Throughout much of that time, the C.Y.C. was running the largest league in the country. In 1966 it

had 447 teams among its divisions from under-eight through adults.

When did the first women's club team come to the United States from a foreign nation for games?

Dick Kerr Limited, an electric company based in Preston, England, sponsored a team of women on a tour of the U.S. in 1922. They played eight men's teams along the East Coast (not always being taken seriously), winning three, tying three, and losing two.

Which was the first club team from the United States to tour Europe?

Thomas Cahill, the secretary of the United States Soccer Federation (then called the United States Football Association), arranged a trip for Bethlehem Steel, of Bethlehem, Pennsylvania, to play several games in Norway and Sweden in 1919. The team, composed primarily of English and Irish immigrants, was the defending U.S. Open Cup champion and later became a charter member of the professional American Soccer League as well as the most successful team in the U.S. during the first quarter of the 20th Century. Bethlehem Steel played 14 games in Europe, winning seven, losing two, and drawing five.

Has the U.S. Men's National Team beaten England any time other than in 1950?

The English were none too happy with the rebellious colonies after 1950. Three years later, England's national team came to New York City to beat us 6-3. It only got worse. In 1959 they took an 8-1 game in Los Angeles to be followed by another win in New York City, 10-0, in 1964. They stayed away until 1985 for a 5-0 win in L.A. Finally the United States beat England in 1993 near the location where the colonies gave King Charles III his first defeat of the American Revolution. England went home from

Foxboro, Massachusetts, beaten 2-0. Thomas Dooley and
Alexi Lalas scored as part of the U.S. Cup, our own
invitational tournament. The two teams met again, in
London in 1994. England won that one 2-0. We both met
in 2005 in Chicago, where England beat us 2-1. Altogether
the stats are England 6, and U.S. 4 (including the American
Revolution and the War of 1812).

**Prior to the United States/England match in the 1950
Men's World Cup, which of the two teams had more
victories in World Cup games?**
Far earlier in this book, I covered some of England's
disagreements with FIFA during the first years of the 20th
Century. By the time England and the global governor of
the game got involved in a long-term commitment, the
World Cups of 1930, 1934, and 1938 were history, leaving
the nation that had invented soccer without one World Cup
game in its past. England started the 1950 World Cup with
a 2-0 victory over Chile, giving it a 1-0-0 record in World
Cup games. The U.S., by contrast, lost its first game of the
1950 World Cup to Spain 3-1. However, with two wins and
a loss from the 1930 World Cup (and a loss during the 1934
tournament), the United States owned one more victory
than England on the day they met in 1950.

**Did the U.S. victory over England knock England out of
the 1950 World Cup?**
To some, this is the biggest upset of the history of the
World Cup. England, after all, invented soccer. The stories
go that the 1-0 upset was so surprising that when
newspaper editors saw it come in from wire reports, the
editors assumed that England's score was a typo; that it
should have been *10*, not *0*. Anyway, the game did not send
England home since it was part of pool play. After that
game England, the United States, and Spain were all
mathematically still alive within the pool of four teams.

Spain had two victories while the U.S. and England had one each. Chile, with two losses, was eliminated. The third round of games pitted the U.S. against Chile and England against Spain. England lost to Spain 1-0, and Chile beat the U.S. 5-2, sending everybody but Spain home.

Who was the first American to play in Germany's top division?

In 1987 Paul Caligiuri seemed to have that honor sewn up as he was earning solid playing time with Hamburg SV during pre-season. Then his team's goalie punched an opponent and was thrown off the team, leaving Coach Josip Skoblar to find a replacement. The coach signed a Yugoslav, putting his likely line-up one too heavy in foreign players. To make room for the 'keeper, Caligiuri, also a foreigner, was sent to a second division team and had to work his way around and back up. In 1995 he played with F.C. St. Pauli in the Bundesliga. By then, however, Eric Wynalda had joined the Bundesliga's Saarbrucken, where in 1992 he played in several games and scored nine goals.

Through 2006 how many times has the U.S. Men's National Team beaten unified Germany?

Germany has been the bearer of bad several times for the U.S. They dealt us a 4-3 defeat in our own tournament, the U.S. Cup, in 1993. They beat us six months later 3-0. The disaster that was the 1998 World Cup started with a 2-0 defeat at the hands of Germany. We lost to them 4-2 in a friendly in 2002, and three months later they ended our 2002 World Cup by beating us 1-0. In 2006 they beat us in a friendly 4-1. We have beaten Germany twice. The first time came in 1999 in Jacksonville, Florida. The 3-0 victory was Bruce Arena's first win as head coach of the team. We beat them 2-0 five months later.

**What about East Germany? How many times did the
United States Men's National Team play them?**
Just prior to there being no more East Germany, the U.S.
took them on twice, both friendlies. We lost 3-2 in East
Berlin in March 1990 and lost again 2-1 four months later
in Milwaukee. East Germany played only one more game
as a separate nation.

**When the United States Men's National Team stepped
on the field to play Italy in the 1934 World Cup why did
Italian Luis Monti look familiar?**
Back then FIFA was a little lenient on the citizenship
requirements. Four years prior to the 1934 World Cup,
Monti had played for Argentina versus the U.S. in the 1930
World Cup. Now FIFA is far more stringent, allowing a
player to appear for only one full national team ever. Youth
teams don't necessarily count.

**How many times has the U.S. Men's National Team
played Italy in Italy during a World Cup?**
Italy hosted the World Cup in 1934 and 1990 and played the
U.S. both times. In 1934 the U.S. fell 7-1. Just prior to the
1990 rematch, Italian Giorgio Chinaglia made two
predictions. He said that soccer's growth in the U.S. would
forever fail "because Americans love sports that involve
hands and eyes." Chinaglia also said that Italy would win
7-0. Italy won 1-0, a score that disappointed many fans and
had them cheering for the Americans during the game.

**What member of the 1992 Men's U.S. Olympic team
turned down an offer to sign with F.C. Barcelona to
return for his sophomore year of college?**
After the U.S. team lost to Italy in Barcelona, the F.C.
Barcelona vice president introduced himself to Claudio
Reyna and asked if the 19-year-old would be interested in
joining the defending European Cup champion. Reyna,

enjoying college at the University of Virginia and wanting to be available for national team camps and games, turned them down.

What unexpected event happened when the U.S. Men's National Team played Olympic in Marseille, France, in 1978?
With the NASL often refusing to give up players for the U.S. National Team, the opportunities for the players to work out together were rare. In fact Ricky Davis was once fined by the St. Louis Steamers for missing a game in order to play a national team friendly against Columbia. Finally getting some cooperation from the players' club teams, U.S. Men's National Team Coach Walt Chyzowych took the team to Europe in mid-1978 to prepare for 1982 World Cup qualifying by playing any team that would host the U.S. men. There the U.S. won a game on European soil for the first time in 34 years. The problem with the victory was that it came against Olympic, a French club dedicating a new stadium by hosting the U.S. When the wrong team won, U.S. Soccer Federation President Gene Edwards had to apologize for ruining the celebration.

How well did France do in qualifying for the 1994 World Cup, the one immediately prior to the World Cup it hosted?
Remember how much FIFA was criticized for its decision to play the 1994 World Cup in the United States, a nation that could not make it through qualifying? A lot of people stood up to complain that FIFA was selling the World Cup and giving the United States an undeserved spot in the 24-team event. This was the series of events: FIFA's decision to play the 1994 World Cup in the U.S., tons of criticism for that decision, the 1990 World Cup in Italy, the decision to play the 1998 World Cup in France, the 1994 World Cup in the U.S., the 1998 World Cup in France. As it turned

out, the U.S. shut some people up by qualifying for the 1990 World Cup, somewhat validating the free pass it would receive in 1994. By contrast, France failed to qualify for the 1994 World Cup, raising questions about whether it deserved the free pass it would get in 1998.

What team prevented France from coming to the 1994 World Cup in the U.S.?
Coming through qualifying, France needed only a tie against Bulgaria in its last game. With the score at 1-1, France gave up a goal in the final minute, sending Bulgaria to the 1994 World Cup. There Bulgaria reached the semifinals while France watched the game on television.

Through 2006 how many times has the U.S. Men's National Team beaten Argentina?
We first played Argentina in 1928, losing 11-2. Two years later they knocked us out of the World Cup, 6-1. We did not play them again until 1975, losing 6-0. We lost to them in 1991, 1-0, and in 2003, 1-0. The only two U.S. victories in the series came in 1995, 3-0, and in 1999, 1-0.

Through 2006 how many times has the U.S. Men's National Team beaten Brazil?
We first played Brazil in 1930, losing 4-3, but did not meet them again until 1992. The most notable of our 12 matches, was in the second round of the 1994 World Cup. Brazil won 1-0. The two teams met a year later and then in 1996, both times Brazil coming out 1-0 winners. In 1998's CONCACAF Gold Cup it went 1-0 again, but with the Americans winning. It is still the only time the U.S. has beaten Brazil. Preki scored the goal, and Kasey Keller proved invincible. Keller had save after amazing save, earning a congratulatory handshake from his opponent after stopping a shot by Brazilian star Romario. After the game

Romario said that he had never seen a better game by any goalkeeper.

And of course this question: how many times has France's Men's National Team beaten the U.S.?

Let's remember that between 1950 and 1990 beating the U.S. Men's National Team put your team in the category of dwarf killers. Yes, France beat us twice, but we let them win to boost their low self-esteem (originally brought on by their faulty-reasoned 18th Century alignment with American Indians to start a war with the U.S. Colonies). Both games were in 1979, ending 6-0 and 3-0.

The U.S. opened up the 2002 World Cup against Luis Figo and Portugal. What individual award had Figo recently won?

Figo played his club soccer with Real Madrid, then the champion club for all Europe. For his play with Real Madrid and the national team, he had earned the honor of 2002 FIFA World Player of the Year.

What was the final score when the U.S. Men's National Team played Poland in the 2002 World Cup?

The U.S. needed to tie for a sure place in the next round. But Poland scored twice before the fifth minute. Landon Donavan put one in the net but had it called back on a crap call before Poland went up 3-0. Donovan did get one on the board later, and Brad Friedel saved a PK. Even though the U.S. lost 3-1, we got through because of South Korea's win over Portugal. The streets of South Korea were relatively happy afterward. Poland's fans were joyful for the win. The American fans were happy to be going through. The Koreans were elated to have won the group, earning a spot in the final 16. Of course Portugal was upset, leaving with three points after arriving as a tournament favorite.

Mexico

After the U.S. beat Mexico to qualify for the 1934 World Cup, how many years passed before the U.S. Men's National Team beat Mexico again?
In hindsight, knowing that we would have to beat Mexico to get to future World Cups, perhaps the U.S. Men's National team should have given in back in 1934. In World Cup qualifying and all other men's national team matches that followed the 1934 game in Italy, Mexico managed to keep us winless until 1982, 48 years later.

Did Mexico qualify for the 1990 World Cup?
It's an odd question for a book about U.S. soccer. But keep in mind that the U.S. competes against Mexico for entry into the World Cup every four years. Mexico did not qualify for the 1990 World Cup because it was suspended by FIFA for using overage players to qualify for the 1989 World Youth Championships. That harsh punishment was suspected by some people as a FIFA ploy to help the U.S. reach the 1990 World Cup. *The Complete Encyclopedia of Soccer* begins a paragraph about U.S. soccer with this phrase: "With Mexico suspended, the U.S. qualified for the 1990 World Cup." It remained a contentious point between the Mexican soccer community and the U.S. soccer community for years even to the point that Mexico's soccer officials perpetuated the rumor that Henry Kissinger helped set up the Mexican coaches who used the overage players. Even when the two teams met in Korea in 2002, the match was seen by some Mexicans as an opportunity for restitution. The Americans won 2-0, but the impression of favoritism dissipated only gradually. The rift continues.

With Mexico out of the way, qualifying for the 1990 World Cup became easier for other CONCACAF teams.

FIFA made another decision that significantly helped the U.S. get in. What was that decision?
FIFA gave the CONCACAF region another slot in the finals, meaning that a second team from North America, Central America, and the Caribbean would advance to Italy. With two openings available and Mexico ineligible to fill either, the U.S. looked ahead to a strong opportunity to return to the world's stage.

What national team benefited the most by Mexico being disqualified from the 1990 World Cup?
The claim that the U.S. was helped by Mexico's disqualification has some holes that become apparent with comprehensive hindsight. At the time that Mexico was removed from qualification, it was in a two-team group with Costa Rica. So, Costa Rica got to go through without having to play Mexico, finding itself in the final round of qualifying with five other teams. Without the disqualification, Costa Rica *or* Mexico would have reached the final round, not both. In that final round the top two teams were granted passage to the World Cup. In that last qualifying round, Costa Rica took the first spot; the U.S. took the second. Had the disqualification never happened, Mexico may have reached the final round, but Mexico and Costa Rica both would not have reached the final round. Had Mexico not been disqualified, the U.S. probably would have qualified. Costa Rica probably would not have.

During qualifying for the 2002 World Cup, Mexico lost to Costa Rica on June 16, 2001. Why was that result so stunning?
Going into the match, Mexico had never lost a game in Mexico City's Azteca stadium. Knowing that history, teams typically pray for a tie when they head into games against Mexico there. In that round of qualifying, Costa

Rica was the only team to score in the stadium, ending up
with a 2-1 victory.

What former Dallas Burn player went on to coach in Mexico?

Hugo Sanchez spent the inaugural season of MLS playing
for Dallas in 23 games. He scored six goals and received
six cautions and one ejection. In 2005 he was coaching
UNAM in Mexico.

What position did Mexico National Team player Jorge Campos play for the L.A. Galaxy in 1996?

This is a bit of a trick question since Campos played two
positions for the team that year. His primary
responsibilities were in the goal. However, ten times
during the season he played as a forward, earning one assist
during the season.

Why didn't Mexico National Team player Cuauhtemoc Blanco travel to the United States for a time after a 2003 visit to Houston?

On May 8, 2003, the men's national teams of the U.S. and
Mexico played in Houston. They tied. After the game,
Blanco allegedly punched a person seeking an autograph.
That person then filed a suit against him but could not get
legal papers served on him in Mexico. Had Blanco
returned to the U.S., specifically to Dallas for a game in
April 2004, he likely would have been served.

Over the course of past games between the national teams of the United States and Mexico, which team has the better record?

There's a line in the Movie *A Shot at Glory* in which the
coach tells his out-classed players not to score early on their
opponents because it may piss off the opponents. That
1934 game between the United States and Mexico seems to

have pissed off the Mexicans. The 1934 World Cup qualifier was the first official meeting between the two neighbors and the first time that qualifiers were used to get into the tournament. Through June 1991, the two teams met during qualifiers, other tournaments, and in friendly matches 27 more times. The U.S. won one of those games, giving Mexico an overall advantage of 22 wins, 2 losses, and 4 ties. The tide turned in July 1991 in a semifinal game of the Gold Cup, the annual tournament for national teams from North America, Central America, and the Caribbean. Coach Bora Milutinovic told his U.S. players, "You're going to win." Eric Wynalda remembered the team looking at the coach and thinking, Are you Crazy? Bora was proven correct as the United States beat Mexico for only the third time in history. Mexico National Team Coach Manuel Lapuente resigned as a result. Until that game, remembered Wynalda in 2005, playing against Mexico was like "standing in the corner with our gloves up taking punches." Starting with that 1991 game, the United States holds a recent advantage through 2005 of 11 wins, 7 losses, and 5 ties.

What is the largest margin of victory the U.S. Men's National Team has had over Mexico?
During the 1995 Nike U.S. Cup, our own invitational tournament for national teams, the U.S. beat Mexico 4-0 in Washington, D.C. We went on to win that tournament seven days later with a tie against Columbia.

When the United States hosted Mexico for a 2002 World Cup qualifier where did they play?
In most World Cup qualifying, FIFA requires that each team in every round host each other team. That doesn't mean that teams have to be gracious hosts; they seldom are. The home field advantage is taken to an extreme. Mexico scheduled its home game versus the U.S. to involve high

altitude, extreme heat, and the smoggiest part of the day. In its own effort to take advantage of the home field, the U.S. Soccer Federation scheduled its home qualifier against Mexico in the first stadium built specifically for a Major League Soccer team. That game brought Mexico to Columbus, Ohio, on a February night. The visitors had to withstand a crowd that was overwhelmingly pro-U.S. while the temperature dipped to the low 20s.

How did the U.S. Men's National Team do against Mexico during the 2002 World Cup?
Brian McBride scored in the eighth minute, and Landon Donavan added another in the 65th. The final score was 2-0, and the U.S. went through to the quarterfinals for the first time since 1930.

Foreigners

In what year did the first club team from a foreign country (not counting Canada) tour the United States?
Seeing an opportunity to promote soccer in the United States, Thomas Cahill organized a tour of amateur players from England in 1905. Calling themselves the Pilgrims, the team played five games in Canada and 12 in the United States against local clubs and citywide all-star teams, generating significant media coverage. Cahill brought a similar group of players back four years later.

What city hosted the amateur championship of the world in 1909?
During the second Pilgrims' tour of the U.S., a team of St. Louis all-stars was selected to play against the Pilgrims for the Cochrane Cup, the trophy held by the amateur champions among England, Ireland, Scotland, Canada, and

the U.S. Only teams with native-born players could compete for it. The Pilgrims won 4-0 in St. Louis.

Which was the first winner of the National Challenge Cup to be completely composed of American-born players?

The second and third decades of the 1900s was a time in St. Louis when a good Sunday could earn professional players $6 each. The Ben Miller Hatters won the city's professional championship in 1916, 1917, 1919, 1920, 1925, 1926, and 1927. The 1920 team won the national championship with a roster of nobody but Americans.

Who was the Manchester United star that the Cosmos tried to bring into the NASL at the same time the team was working to bring in Pele?

After 37 appearances with the Northern Ireland Men's National Team and several years with Manchester United, George Best talked with the Cosmos about joining the NASL and went so far as to give the team a verbal commitment in 1975. The 1968 European Footballer of the Year was also a heavy drinker, leading to suspensions from Manchester United and trouble from the later teams he played for. Three times Best had announced in 1972 and 1973 that he was retiring. Each time, he changed his mind. After committing to the Cosmos, he signed with the Los Angeles Aztecs in late 1975, carrying his global celebrity to the West Coast. The media followed him on and off the field. He moved to the Ft. Lauderdale Strikers in 1978 and then to the San Jose Earthquakes, a stint that lasted until August 1981. In his 150 NASL games he scored 57 goals and had 60 assists. Brandi Chastain went to the Earthquakes camps as a youngster and attended several games. She idolized Best as a player and wrote that he is probably the reason she started playing soccer as a striker.

Why was Franz Beckenbauer's decision to come to the NASL such a boost to the league?
When Pele and George Best signed on to play in the NASL, they were coming out of retirement. The league had the image of being for aged stars and lower level European youngsters looking to earn good money. Beckenbauer won the World Cup with West Germany in 1974 and was named European Player of the Year in 1976. When he came to the NASL, in 1977, he was still at the top of his game. Teammate Shep Messing wrote in his 1978 book, "There is no doubt that Franz is the finest player alive."

What happened in Germany that made Franz Beckenbauer leave for the New York Cosmos?
During 1975 and 1976, representatives of the Cosmos talked to Beckenbauer about leaving Bayern Munich. In January 1977, he decided to wait until after the 1978 World Cup to make the move. Three months after that decision, on April 6, 1977, *Die Welt*, a German newspaper, ran a story about Beckenbauer's private life, claiming that the Kaiser was guilty of adultery, tax evasion, bankrupting his club, and betraying his national team. The next three weeks were "days of pure horror for me and my family," he said. Looking to get away from that horror, the 31-year-old Beckenbauer went ahead and joined the Cosmos. He said that he would have stayed in Germany "if the press campaign had not taken place."

Who is the only person to win three World Cups as a player and to play in the North American Soccer League?
Only one person has played on three World Cup-winning teams, and I gave away his name earlier in this book. At 17 years old, Pele came off the bench in 1958 to help Brazil win its first. He and the team repeated in 1962. The Brazilian government considered him so vital to the nation,

that it named him a national treasurer, thus non-exportable. That forbade his club, Santos, from following the trend of South American teams selling their players to European clubs. What seemed to be a disadvantage to his club turned out to reap great rewards, though. Santos embarked on regular foreign tours with Pele, generating tons of cash. After leading Brazil's national team to the World Cup title in 1970, he became even more sought after as Santos kept booking games in other countries. When he retired from the national team in July 1971, his club games were the only way to catch him in action until he retired from Santos in October 1974. During his final game with Santos, Pele caught the ball and then shook hands with players, referees, and coaches. He took a lap around the stadium and jogged out the tunnel to a car. People around the world mourned at the thought of never seeing him play again. To get him back on the field, Henry Kissinger and the U.S. Government arranged for education assistance from the Cosmos to schools in Brazil, and Cosmos executives pitched the advantages of Pele's children growing up in the U.S. The Brazilian government relented, and Pele decided to join the NASL.

In 1972 the NASL started mandating that two players on each team's roster have a certain distinction. What was that distinction?
The teams from St. Louis and Philadelphia stood out in the league because of their reliance on American talent. Meanwhile most teams focused on winning games with whichever players they could get their hands on. In an effort to lure Americans to appreciate the game, the league decided that each team should have at least two players from the U.S. or Canada on its 18-man roster. That minimum would increase each year by one.

Did the NASL ever mandate what nationalities should actually be on the field?
Starting in 1979 each team had to have at least two Americans on the field. Then it was three for 1980 and 1981, and four for '82 and '83.

Of all the people who have come and gone in the history of the world, how many have played on a team that won the World Cup and on a team that won one of the first 11 MLS Cups?
These words here were written to keep your eyes from inadvertently spotting the answer before you finish reading the question, which can be answered with this word: zero. Both of these fraternities of players are quite small. The only real chance of overlap in membership comes from the three players who joined MLS teams after playing for national teams that won World Cup titles. First there was Branco, who played for the MetroStars in 1997 after winning the World Cup with Brazil in 1994. Then came Lothar Matthaus, World Cup winner with West Germany. He played for the MetroStars in 2000. In 2005 Youri Djorkaeff signed with, you guessed it, the MetroStars. He had been part of France's national team that won the cup in 1998. None of those MetroStars teams won an MLS Cup. Come to think of it, no MetroStars teams have won an MLS Cup.

What about an NASL championship? Has anybody been on a team that won the World Cup and on a team that won the NASL title?
These words here were written to keep your eyes …. The answer is yes. The most notable winner of both is Pele with Brazil (1958, 1962, and 1970) and with the New York Cosmos (1977). Franz Beckenbauer did it with West Germany in 1974 and the Cosmos three times. Alan Ball, after winning the World Cup with England in 1966, won

the NASL crown with Vancouver in 1979. Notably, none of them won the World Cup after their experience in the NASL. Their days of winning the greatest title on the planet were behind them when they joined the NASL.

Who was the second best player to come into the NASL in 1975?
While being seen by many in the United States for the first time, Eusebio scored nine goals during the 1966 World Cup, four of them to bring Portugal back from a three-goal deficit against North Korea. His career also included being named European Player of the Year and leading Portugal's domestic league in scoring during the five seasons of 1964 through 1968. He joined the NASL's Boston Minutemen just weeks after Pele had come to the U.S. He went to Toronto for the following season. There he led the team to a Soccer Bowl victory over Minnesota 3-0. The next year he played for the Las Vegas Quicksilvers, his last team before giving in to injuries and ending his career.

True of False: The United States Men's National Team that played in the 1950 World Cup included eight players who had played professionally in England?
This is a myth that sprouted from a complaint from the English Football Association and has been perpetuated by fans of England's national team, the same team that got upset by the U.S. in that tournament. In truth, the United States' team was a collection of players who for the most part had been born and raised in the states. Most were second-generation Americans. There were a few exceptions, particularly Joe Gaetjens, Joe Maca, and Ed McIlvenny. They were not U.S. citizens but had filed "first papers", declarations of their intent to become citizens. Following the tournament, Maca did become a U.S. citizen, but the other two did not. As for England's complaint, FIFA heard it on December 2, 1950, and dismissed it.

What was Canada's basis for protesting its March 1997 loss to the United States during 1998 World Cup qualifying?
During his tenure as U.S. coach, Steve Sampson brought in several players by getting them to become U.S. citizens. Preki was one. David Regis was another. For the game against Canada, David Wagner and Michael Mason, both born and raised in Germany and both playing in Germany's top division, appeared for the first time in a U.S. uniform. Their citizenship was based on each having one American parent. They both figured in the U.S. goals that day, and inspired Canada to claim that Wagner was ineligible due to prior appearances with Germany's national teams. Wagner was used to such questions since there was another player of the same name in Germany.

We know that the NASL required a minimum number of American players on its teams. What about MLS? Does it do likewise?
As evidence of how the soccer environment has changed, Major League Soccer does not set a minimum for American players; it sets a maximum for foreign players. With its inaugural season in 1996, the league allowed five foreigners on each team's roster. That number was dropped to four for the 1999 season. Even though the policy did not restrict the nationalities of the players on the field, when the 2003 championship game began between San Jose and Chicago, 18 of the 22 starters were Americans.

Who's this? He has played in more games of the Men's World Cup than any other man and he has played in Major League Soccer.
At the close of the 1988 World Cup, Lothar Matthaus had played in 25 World Cup games. That included France in 1998, the U.S. in 1994, Italy in 1990, and Mexico in 1986. In 2000 he was added to the roster of the New York/New

Jersey MetroStars. When he arrived in the States, he first lived in an apartment that had been furnished by the team. Wanting something more suited to his taste, Matthaus ordered new furniture and sent the bill to the team. He lasted 21 games with the MetroStars.

Who played for the Kansas City Wizards after breaking the Catholic barrier with Scotland's Rangers?

The rift between Rangers and Celtic in Scotland is volatile. Rangers is supported by Protestants while Celtic is strictly Catholic. A slight break in tradition came in 1989, when Mo Johnston became the first Catholic since World War II to play for Rangers. Johnston joined Kansas City in 1996.

How many times was Branco ejected from MetroStars' games?

Three years after helping Brazil win the 1994 World Cup, Branco joined the New York/New Jersey MetroStars for 11 games. He received three ejections.

In 2004 the United Soccer Leagues' PDL division had a player named Jay Goppingen on the Orange County Blue Star team. What country was he from?

After retiring from pro soccer in 1998, Juergen Klinsmann, the former German superstar, moved to Southern California. Klinsmann's career had included being part of West Germany's team that won the 1990 World Cup. He also was part of Germany's 1994 and 1998 teams that made it to the World Cup quarterfinals. Living in California, Klinsmann found himself with some free time, encouraging him to join the Orange County team. His fake last name comes from the German town where he grew up.

Travel

Why did Earnie Stewart leave Portland, Maine, so quickly after helping the U.S. Men's National Team's beat Costa Rica in a World Cup qualifier in September 1997?
Just recently FIFA implemented a worldwide calendar that specifies dates when club teams and national teams have precedence over each other. The calendar gives clubs notice of the dates that players should be available for national team games. National teams are permitted to play outside those dates but cannot expect cooperation from club teams. Doing double duty creates significant problems when players are traveling from one continent to another, like Earnie Stewart did in 1997. After Stewart helped the U.S. beat Costa Rica in Portland, Maine, taking a step closer to the 1998 World Cup, he hopped on a plane to return to the Netherlands. Not more than 24 hours after finishing the game in Portland, he stepped on the field and scored the only goal for NAC Breda in its victory over Maastricht.

Forty hours after the United States Men's National Team lost to Germany in the 2002 World Cup, what was Landon Donovan doing?
In that quarterfinal match Donovan had a shot that would have gone in had the German goalkeeper clipped his fingernails that morning. Nevertheless, Donovan found himself back in San Jose less than two whole days later playing for the San Jose Earthquakes. By comparison, the U.S. team that played in the 1930 World Cup in Uruguay, South America, traveled by ship and was out of the country for three months.

After the U.S. Men's National Team got knocked out of the 2002 World Cup, Pablo Mastroeni headed back to

the U.S. to play for his club team, the MetroStars. What did he do that made him stand out in his first game back?

Mastroeni, who played in three games in South Korea (including 80 minutes against Germany), flew from Seoul to L.A. to Phoenix. The next day he flew to New York. Twenty minutes into his first game back, he got ejected.

Among all the domestic soccer leagues in the world, which one has the farthest distance among two of its teams?

Every season the New England Revolution and the L.A. Galaxy meet a few times during the Major League Soccer season. Since 2005 New England and Chivas USA have been matching up as well. Each time, one team has to travel the 3,026 miles between Boston and L.A., the greatest distance between any two teams of a domestic league.

What foreign country had a team that offered American Billy Gonsalves a professional contract?

After starring for the U.S. in the 1930 and 1934 World Cups, Billy Gonsalves received an offer to play in Brazil for Botafogo. Buff Donelli, after playing for the U.S. in the 1934 cup, was offered a spot with Italian Lazio. Both turned down the offers.

What was so odd about the weather for the first U.S. game of the 1930 World Cup?

Played in Uruguay, the tournament took place during the Southern Hemisphere's winter, actually the middle of winter. The U.S.'s first game, against Belgium, was played on July 13th. As the players walked onto the field, snow fell.

Through 2006, how many times has the U.S. Men's National Team beaten a South American national team in South America?

The most significant two victories of this type came during the 1995 Copa America, the championship for national teams from South America with a few other nations invited. The U.S. opened the tournament, held in Uruguay, by beating Chile 2-1. After a 1-0 loss to Bolivia, The U.S. beat defending champion Argentina 3-0 and went on to place fourth in the tournament. In 2000 the U.S. added a third victory over a South American team on South American soil by defeating Chile in Chile 2-1.

Of the 23 men on the U.S. roster for the 2002 World Cup, where did more of the players play their club soccer, in Europe or in the U.S.?

It's an amazing question considering that just 12 years earlier many of the U.S. players were not playing club soccer. They had gone straight from college to the national team. By 2002, however, the United States was producing players with the skills to reach the top leagues in the world and keep a domestic league afloat. During the 2002 tournament, 12 held day-jobs in Europe while 11 suited up for MLS teams.

What was the earliest year that the U.S. Men's National Team got anything better than a loss in Mexico City against Mexico?

In 1965 we came close. During a World Cup qualifier on March 12, we had two goals called back and ended up losing 2-0. It would have been a huge upset, tying Mexico in Mexico City. To that date, the best we had done in Mexico City was a 3-1 loss. What was even more startling about the two goals being called back is that both were scored by Willy Roy. One was called back for offside; the other for a handball. Not until November 4, 1997, did we get anything as good as a tie. The referees did not help in that one either, sending off Jeff Agoos in the first half. Nevertheless we held on 0-0 and got one point toward qualifying for the 1998 World Cup.

In what country did executives of the New York Cosmos first talk with Pele about playing in the United States?
The head of the New York Cosmos, Clive Toye, met Pele in Jamaica as he relaxed near a hotel pool during a Santos team tour. There, Toye first breached the subject of Pele joining the New York Cosmos after retiring from Santos. Pele thought he was joking.

Crossing the Pond

When was the first time that Manchester United played in the United States?
Manchester United came to the U.S. and Canada for the first time to play 12 games in 1950. The team has returned a few times since. On one of those return trips, in 1976, ManU visited Dallas to play the Tornado of the NASL and witnessed where the league had taken soccer. General Manager Dick Berg used many entertaining gimmicks to appeal to fans, including a monkey that warmed up his goalkeepers. The monkey had another skill, climbing along the crossbar whenever the Tornado scored a goal. Since the Manchester United Game in Dallas finished 2-2, the Brits watched the monkey celebrate on the crossbar twice.

Of their 12 games against Canadian teams, U.S. club teams, and U.S. all-star teams during that 1950 tour, how many did ManU win?
Along with two losses and two ties, Manchester won eight. Their closest game from a U.S. club team came from the St. Louis's Joe Simpkins team, the U.S. Open Cup champions.

Without conceding any goals, Manchester scored five on goalkeeper Frank Borghi. Two months later, though, Borghi got his revenge by being far stingier against some Englishmen. Borghi became the goalkeeper for the U.S. team that went to the 1950 World Cup and played against England. In that game he refused every shot from all English players, allowing the U.S. to win 1-0.

Fabien Barthez led France's national team to the World Cup title in 1998 and the European Championship in 2000. He led his club team, Manchester United, to Premier League championships in 2001 and 2003. Who replaced him in 2003 as Manchester United's goalkeeper?

Barthez had blundered a couple times before United picked up American Tim Howard in the summer of 2003. Nevertheless, Howard, living beyond his dreams, had no assurance of starting ahead of Barthez on the world's most popular team. Howard's hopes got a boost when Barthez made a goof worthy of wacky highlight films. In a pre-season friendly, Barthez watched the ball get chipped over his head from 35 yards out. The crossbar prevented a goal, but as Barthez retreated, the ball rebounded off his head, sending it into the net.

Who is the only American to play in the field for Manchester United?

He was born in Illinois but after some time in Manchester United's youth system, Jonathan Spector, a defender, got into an English Premier League match in 2004 for United. In his second game, against Everton, he was named Man of the Match.

Who was the first American to play in Italy's top division, Serie A?

During the U.S. men's games of the 1994 World Cup, a red

head with a long goatee got the attention of professional coaches throughout the globe. After the tournament, Alexi Lalas signed with Italian club Padova, where he took the nickname *Buffalo Bill* because of their similar looks. When MLS started up in 1996, Lalas, arguably the most recognizable U.S. player, returned to the states to play for New England. Referring to his marketing impact, MLS Deputy Commissioner Sunil Gulati called Lalas "the most important player-signing for this league."

In his third start for Sheffield Wednesday, what legendary goalie did John Harkes score on?

Playing against Derby County in December 1990 in a league cup match, Harkes scored on Peter Shilton from a little more than 30 yards. Shilton was also the England National Team starting goalkeeper and had become the most-capped goalkeeper in the world. Shilton allowed another goal in that game, one which Harkes assisted, helping the American earn man of the match honors in Wednesday's 2-1 win. The game had started oddly for Harkes, who was still getting settled far from home. After Harkes had asked for a long-sleeve jersey to keep him warm, his manager responded by giving him a shot of brandy. Harkes drank it just seconds before starting the game. Then he scored the goal that he later called the turning point in his soccer career.

Who was the first American to play in a League Cup final in England?

In England, soccer's top three trophies are for winning the weekly schedule among league opponents, the tournament among all Football Association teams (known as the FA Cup), and the lesser tournament among teams in the top F.A. divisions (known as the League Cup). In 1991 John Harkes' team, Sheffield Wednesday, marched through the League Cup tournament to the final, earning him the honor as the first American to play in the prestigious final. Wednesday's 1-0 win over powerhouse Manchester United made Harkes the first American to earn a League Cup championship. It was the club's first championship in fifty-six years.

Who was the first American to score in a League Cup final in England?

Harkes and his Sheffield teammates returned to the League Cup Final in 1993, to play Arsenal. Wednesday lost 2-1, but Harkes recorded the first goal ever scored by an American in the League Cup final. Even more startling is that the goal was scored on David Seaman, then the current national team goalkeeper for England.

Who was the first American to play in a Football Association cup final in England?

This is the tournament of football tournaments in England. Several hundred teams start out in this mega-March Madness. Because of the number of teams competing, it is traditionally considered more prestigious than the League Cup. Again the answer is John Harkes, who played with Sheffield Wednesday in the team's 1993 loss to Arsenal.

Who was England's 2003 Goalkeeper of the Year?

Pele told a reporter in 1975 that he expected the first globally known American soccer player would be a goalkeeper. How do you compare goalkeepers to field players, though? It's really apples and oranges when you are talking about contributions to a team's success. Be that as it may, the first American to receive a major award in a foreign league was Brad Friedel, who was playing in goal for Blackburn in 2003, when he was chosen England's Goalkeeper of the Year.

Who's this? In 1994 he left Southern California at age 16 to join the youth system of Ajax in Amsterdam, Holland. He started playing with the first division team four years later and won league titles with that team. Pitted against the best teams of the continent's other national leagues, this player helped Ajax to the quarterfinals of the Champions League.
He also scored the U.S.'s first goal of the 2002 World Cup and played every minute of the tournament. He's John O'Brien.

Cosmos

What were the three primary reasons that had Pele deciding to join the New York Cosmos?
In Harry Harris' biography of Pele, he notes that the contract with the Cosmos enabled Pele to pay off all his debts and make a significant profit. The second reason was that he saw the contribution he would be making to the game by boosting its image in the United States. The third reason was the programs that the Cosmos agreed to conduct in Brazil dealing with poverty and education.

What video game system helped fund the New York Cosmos?
The company behind *The Exorcist, The Swarm, MAD Magazine,* Asylum records, and Atari video games was Warner Communications, also the owner of the New York Cosmos. Atari games were big-time sellers. As the middle 80s crept in, however, Warner Communications suffered greatly as competitors entered the video game market. The company reigned in the checkbook and sold 60 percent of the team to Giorgio Chinaglia and a group of investors. It was downhill from there.

In what year did the New York Cosmos fold?
The team began in January 1971 with the prompting of the
NASL, which really, really, really wanted a presence in the
media center of the U.S. Pele joined the club, and he and
his band of world stars set out to win championships and to
tour the world making money. Those tours became a
greater focus in the late 1970s as the Cosmos played against
some of the world's best clubs unconcerned about winning
or losing, paying more attention to attendance and
television contracts. Soon after joining the team in 1976,
Giorgio Chinaglia told Shep Messing about "big plans, for
me, for the Cosmos, for American soccer." Owning 60
percent of the team in 1984, Chinaglia became president
and presided over a decline that poorly reflected the life of
the team but was truly caused by the team's lavish past.
With high payroll and decreasing revenue, the Cosmos—
the team that had given the NASL legitimacy—was
expelled by the league for financial reasons. Having a
handful of players under contract and contact with
European players interested in earning extra money,
Chinaglia scheduled a series of summer games against
foreign teams at Giants Stadium in 1985. The Cosmos had
thrived with big names and found that their fans had grown
to expect stars; less was a second-rate product. Using
unknown players as his base, Chinaglia made deals with
Europeans to join the Cosmos for all or part of the 11-game
summer series. Few of the newcomers had recognizable
names and looked like a team of pick-up gamers wanting
exposure and money. The first two games drew small
crowds, a total of 32,200. The third, played in heavy rain,
drew worse. Taking on Lazio, from Italy, the Cosmos were
watched by 8,677 fans. Additionally harmful was a very
physical game that involved two ejections and an on-field
scuffle. The global soccer scene of 1985 already had
brought several injuries and deaths to fans. The Lazio
match made the Cosmos look no better than what much of

the world was criticizing. And it left the few Cosmos fans making excuses for their continued support. Over the course of the next week, the players complained that they were not being paid, and the fourth game, against a group of West German all-stars, looked to be in jeopardy. Franz Beckenbauer reported that he would miss the next game due to a family commitment, and two team executives quit. Chinaglia responded by flying to Rome and telling reporters that the remaining games would not be played. Likely, he said, the Cosmos would never play again. The team didn't. Chinaglia then turned sour on the United States, saying in 1990 that soccer would never take hold in the United States, predicting that the U.S. would loose to Italy 7-0 in the World Cup, and encouraging FIFA to reconsider its decision to play the 1994 World Cup in the U.S.

Who's this? He joined the New York Cosmos at the start of the 1978 NASL season after playing one season in college at Santa Clara. He played for the Cosmos until 1984, appearing in 154 NASL games and participating in the Cosmos' worldwide exhibition tours while winning NASL titles in 1978, 1980, and 1982. He played in the Major Indoor Soccer League three seasons for the St. Louis Steamers, one for the New York Arrows, and three for the Tacoma Stars.
Before all that, Ricky Davis played his first game for the United States Men's National team on September 15, 1977, against El Salvador. Following the retirement of Werner Roth in 1979, Davis clearly was the outstanding American player among the Cosmos' galaxy of international stars. Through the next decade he was the most prominent American player at both club and national team levels. He played for the United States in the qualifying rounds of the 1982, 1986, and 1990 World Cups. In all, he appeared for the U.S. in 36 full international games, a record at that time,

and scored seven goals. From 1984 onward, he was the
regular captain of the national team.

How long did it take Ricky Davis to score a goal in his first game as a member of the U.S. Men's National Team?

In his first appearance with the U.S. Men's National Team,
Ricky Davis scored against El Salvador just six minutes
into that game. He became a regular with the national team
and the U.S. Olympic Team, leading it in the 1984 and
1988 Olympic Games. Perhaps his best game for the
United States was a 3-0 victory over Costa Rica in the 1984
Olympics, in which he scored two goals in front of what
was then the largest crowd ever to see a soccer game in the
United States, 78,265 people.

How many World Cup games did Ricky Davis appear in for the United States?

Davis was the voice in the wind for soccer in the United
States for several years. During the gray ages, those years
between NASL's end and MLS's beginning, Davis was the
only real recognizable U.S.-born soccer player. A March
1985 Sports Illustrated story focused on him and his dream
of reaching the World Cup. He played for the U.S. Men's
National Team in qualifiers for the World Cups of 1982 and
1986 without success. After playing in the first two
qualifying games for the 1990 World Cup, Davis suffered a
knee injury. As Davis rehabbed his knee, his teammates
qualified for the 1990 World Cup. But when the roster was
named several months later, Coach Bob Gansler left Davis
off the team that went to Italy. He never again played for
the national team.

Indoor

In what year did the NASL stage its first indoor soccer tournament?
Primarily a foul-weather training tool, soccer indoor was what brought teams of the International Soccer League to Chicago in the 1920s. The American Soccer League put together matches in Madison Square Garden in 1939, 1940, and 1958. In 1950 the International Soccer League (after it was renamed the National Soccer League) held a full season of indoor soccer. Indoor soccer was truly kept alive, though, by amateur and youth teams matching up against each other informally in basements and gymnasiums with ever-changing rules concerning the use of walls and the number of players. In 1971 the NASL held an indoor tournament for its teams, won by Dallas Tornado.

With April 1978 as the target, one man announced plans to start the Super Soccer League, a national professional indoor soccer league, in the U.S. What did the Harlem Globetrotters have to do with this plan?
The person behind those plans was Jerry Saperstein, son of the Globetrotters' founder Abe Saperstein. Looking for a money-making vehicle involving sports, Jerry first tried to get a hockey franchise in Florida. Failing that, he ventured into indoor soccer, planning a season to run from April 1978 through November.

How many leagues were there for professional indoor soccer in 1979 in the U.S.?
Similar to the start of an outdoor league in the U.S., professional indoor soccer leagues began as competing groups sought profit. In addition to Jerry Saperstein's Super Soccer League, two other groups announced in 1977 plans to start leagues in 1978. However, the Super Soccer League never got underway. The Major Indoor Soccer

League started in December 1978 with six teams and returned in 1979. The North American Soccer League, having held a few indoor tournaments, offered an indoor schedule to its teams to begin in December 1979.

Of the indoor leagues of the NASL and the original MISL, which one lasted longer?
Having played indoor seasons that ended in 1980, 1981, and 1982, the NASL began seeing disagreements about the indoor game among its own franchises. Of the league's 24 teams, 14 did not participate in the first NASL indoor season. Of the 10 that did, several drew more fans to their indoor games than outdoor games. Some of those franchise owners, seeing the differences in their bottom lines between indoor and outdoor, would have preferred to sit out the outdoor season. The NASL prohibited that, though, and decided not to hold an indoor season for 1982-83. That led some NASL teams to jump to the MISL and contributed to the demise of the NASL and the rise of the MISL. The MISL's triumph over the NASL was short-lived. It, too, folded, but had its name resurrected years later.

What outdoor soccer organization that exists today began as a five-team indoor league?
Led by Francisco Marcos, the Southwest Indoor Soccer League started in 1986 with teams in Albuquerque, New Mexico; Amarillo, Texas; Garland, Texas; Lubbock, Texas; and Oklahoma City, Oklahoma. It added teams and an outdoor schedule, gradually giving up indoor soccer. The number of teams grew so much that the league split into different divisions and was renamed a couple times until it settled on United Soccer Leagues. It now governs several of the leagues below Major League Soccer.

What did the first version of Major Indoor Soccer League change its name to?

The MISL was the soccer league with the most clout after the collapse of the NASL. Granted, the MISL was partially to blame for the demise of professional outdoor soccer. Without the MISL soccer's landscape in the U.S. would have included little more than local teams, colleges, and regional semi-pro leagues through the 1990s. Seeing it as the major league of soccer, executives changed the name to Major Soccer League before the 1990-91 season and began working toward offering an outdoor season.

What team won the first four titles of the original Major Indoor Soccer League?

After luring away Shep Messing from the NASL, the New York Arrows drew attention for its stout defense. But it also had Steve Zungul and Julie Veee as constant scoring threats. The Arrows won the title of the 1978-79 season and the titles for the seasons that ended in 1980, 1981, and 1982. During the last two seasons of that run, Zungul scored 211 goals.

During what year did the Major Indoor Soccer League (a.k.a Major Soccer League) quit operating?

Seemingly every soccer league's rise in the U.S. has come at the expense of another league. When the MISL started in 1978, it hurt the NASL. After the 1991-92 season the MISL fell apart, suffering at the hands of other indoor leagues by competing for attendance, exposure, and talent. In turn, those indoor leagues suffered when Major League Soccer started up in 1996.

What team won the most titles in the original MISL?

The same team won the final five titles of MISL, the San Diego Sockers. It had won three previous titles, giving it eight (1983, 1985, 1986, 1988, 1989, 1990, 1991, and 1992) in the league's 14 years.

**What changes did the American Indoor Soccer
Association make to scoring?**
The American Indoor Soccer Association began in 1984 in
markets typically smaller than MISL cities. It kept costs
down while expanding to other cities. In an effort to
increase excitement, league administrators altered the rules
on scoring in 1988, providing two-point and three-point
goals. In an effort to compete with the MISL, the AISA
was renamed the National Professional Soccer League in
1990. When the MISL folded, that league's franchises from
Wichita, Cleveland, St. Louis, and Baltimore came into the
AISA/NPSL. Suffering from the start-up of MLS, the
AISA/NPSL folded in 2001 to be reborn as the Major
Indoor Soccer League. This second version of MISL exists
today.

**Who was the Washington Warthogs' female player in
1995?**
Looking to keep her skills up and without the Women's
United Soccer Association in operation yet, Kristine Lilly
spent the 1995 season as the only female player in the
Continental Indoor Soccer League, a men's league. She
played with the Warthogs. Lilly had another reason to keep
playing: her grandmother had long earlier started paying her
a dollar for each goal she scored.

Outdoor Leagues

**What two events ended the Golden Age of American
soccer?**
Before there was pro football and just after pro baseball
was taking root in the east, the American Soccer League
started up in 1921, lasting until the Soccer War and the
Great Depression killed it. As a group of players, coaches,
and investors, the ASL saw itself as the money-spending,

risk-taking branch of the game in the U.S. Therefore, they believed, their efforts should not be hampered by the national organization, the U.S. Football Association, which expected ASL teams to play in the annual challenge cup to crown a champion among all professional and amateur teams in the country. Seeing the cup as a hindrance, the ASL decided to bag the tournament of 1924-25. Then the league improperly brought in foreign players and penalized its teams that went ahead and played in the national cup competition. As a consequence, the national body suspended the ASL, making it an outlaw league, and started its own league from the three teams that had been fined by the ASL. The competing leagues were financial cannibals to each other. A weaker ASL continued but got hit by the Great Depression. The league's players had full-time jobs and were forced to go where and when money could be made. At the same time, with attendance slumping, the players had less to gain from staying on the team. Meanwhile, the town factories that supported several of the teams went through tough times as well. Pro baseball suffered but survived. Soccer could not. With fewer people in the stands, the ASL folded after the 1932-33 season. Soccer historian Dave Litterer wrote that the end of the original ASL "marked the end of the golden age of American Soccer."

How many different leagues used the name American Soccer League?

The earliest version actually lured English players to it and was covered regularly by *Soccer Pictorial Weekly*. It began in 1921 and lasted into 1933. That same year, 1933, the second American Soccer League (ASL II) started up, including some of the teams from the first ASL. ASL III came about in 1988 and became part of the American Professional Soccer League after two seasons.

In terms of years existing, what has been the most successful professional soccer league in the United States?

It lasted for 50 years but is hardly memorable. The second version of the American Soccer League started from the ashes of the first version in 1933 as little more than an ethnic-based, East Coast league. Teams relied on local talent with low payrolls while focusing on revenue generated by hosting foreign teams on American tours. Operating during the lowest depths of U.S. interest in the game, the ASL truly was the savior of the game, paying players part-time salaries based on games played and attendance at those games. The league lasted for so long by being so conservative: but it died because it was so conservative. When the United States Soccer Federation granted top-level professional status to the United Soccer Association in 1967, the ASL took notice. After the newer league merged into the NASL, the ASL became a second-rate league, prompting touring clubs to turn their backs on the ASL. The league expanded west and hired basketball star Bob Causey as its commissioner in the 1970s but closed its doors after the 1983 season.

In 1960 in New York City, Kilmarnock, of Scotland, and Bangu, of Brazil, played for a league title. Which league?

Bill Cox played one game for the freshmen soccer team of Yale and went on to work as an executive in professional football and baseball. In 1960 he launched the International Soccer League, bringing foreign teams to the U.S. to play two, six-team schedules. With one U.S. team participating, Cox, brought in clubs from England, Scotland, Ireland, Germany, and France to compete for one spot in the championship game. Then he brought in teams from Italy, Sweden, Yugoslavia, Austria, Portugal, and Brazil to compete for the second spot. Playing all the games in the

New York Area, he got some of the games televised locally. The winner of the first half of the season, Kilmarnock, played Bangu, the winner of the second half, in August in New York's Polo Grounds for the final. Bangu won 2-0.

How many seasons did the International Soccer League play?

After the 1960 season, the league added venues in other U.S. cities to further its revenue base. Meanwhile Dukla (from Czechoslovakia) won championships in 1961, 1962, and 1963. After its fourth season, the league ended, absent the novelty from its earlier days in New York and without sufficient revenues from games in other cities.

In 1966 the United States had no national professional soccer league. What red-letter event that year helped launch two leagues in 1967?

FIFA placed the 1966 World Cup in England, coupling a wave of televised sports with a tournament being hosted by an English-speaking ally. *The New York Times* covered games almost daily while Madison Square Garden and other venues showed several matches on closed circuit television. The extra-time final between England and West Germany was broadcasted live on NBC on a Saturday afternoon. American interest in the 1966 World Cup led several U.S. businessmen to start the two leagues that later became the NASL. One of the people who later joined the NASL, Ricky Davis, watched that 1966 tournament via television and became fascinated by the play of West Germany's Franz Beckenbauer. After signing with the New York Cosmos in 1977, he found his locker next to Beckenbauer's.

How many groups announced plans to start operating professional soccer leagues in 1967 in the United States?

In addition to the two leagues that later merged into the

NASL, a third group announced plans to form a professional soccer league in the United States. It barely got further than the announcement. The other two, the National Professional Soccer League and the United Soccer Association, played separate seasons in 1967. The NPSL had a CBS contract but not the sanction of the United States Soccer Federation. The USA had no national television carrier but USSF blessing. Both hoped to be the Starbucks of sports, launching a trend to make money in an area that had never before succeeded. The financial difficulties were realized immediately, encouraging the two leagues to merge for the 1968 season as the North American Soccer League.

Among the two leagues, the United Soccer Association and the National Professional Soccer League, how many Americans played on their teams?
First off the USA did not even attempt to recruit Americans. Running behind as they tried to capitalize on popular interest in soccer, league organizers imported whole teams from foreign cities for the 1967 season. The Vancouver Royal Canadians were actually the club from Sunderland, England. The New York Skyliners were from Cerro, Uruguay. The competing league, the NPSL, had Americans on its team—a grand total of six among its 179 players.

In 1967 how many North American municipal areas had two top-level pro soccer teams?
With both of them claiming to be North America's top-level pro soccer league in 1967, the United Soccer Association and the National Professional Soccer League had a total of 22 teams. Ten of them were playing in five metropolitan areas: Toronto, Chicago, L.A., New York, and San Francisco-Oakland.

How many teams did the NASL have in 1969?
After the 1968 season, the first after the merger, was played

with 17 teams in 17 cities, the NASL lost Boston, New York, Washington, Chicago, Cleveland, Detroit, Toronto, Houston, Los Angeles, Oakland, San Diego, and Vancouver. That left five teams: Atlanta, Baltimore, Dallas, Kansas City, and St. Louis. Without playoffs, Kansas City won the league because of a convoluted points system. The traditional system of two points for a win and one point for a tie would have put Atlanta on top.

How many teams did the NASL have in 1970?
Baltimore folded. However, teams in Rochester (New York) and Washington D.C. started up. That put the total at six. Washington, of course, would later have a huge presence in MLS. Rochester, though, never got into the top league that started in 1996. Instead Rochester continues to do quite well at the secondary level. The Raging Rhinos won the U.S. Open Cup in 1999, beating four MLS teams during the tournament, and exceeds the attendance of some MLS teams year in and year out. Three times since 1996 the team has won league championships, and it has finished second another two times.

How many teams did the NASL have in 1971?
Of the six from 1970, Kansas City dropped out. However, with the addition of New York, Montreal, and Toronto, the league had a net gain of two teams to start the season at eight.

What was the final season that NASL played games?
In 1984 the league played a season with nine teams, a result of financial problems that had diminished it from 24 teams in 1978, 1979, and 1980. For the 1985 season, four teams continued to exist. Tampa Bay then fell out, and the Cosmos were dropped for missing financial deadlines. The two remaining clubs, Toronto and Minnesota, gave in, and the league called it a day on March 28, 1985.

What national soccer league started competing with the NASL in 1978?
During the 1930s Madison Square Garden had been used for indoor soccer. Sporadically throughout the world, soccer continued to be altered occasionally to a weatherproof environment on a durable surface. It was typically a recreational activity, not a professional pursuit. With enthusiastic soccer communities and indoor arenas available, some northern cities saw the opportunity to alter the game and dive into pro soccer without shelling out the money that NASL teams were going through. This latest Americanization was the Major Indoor Soccer League that was really a cross between hockey and soccer. The league's six teams were located in Philadelphia, Cincinnati, Houston, Pittsburgh, suburban Cleveland, and suburban New York.

How did the NASL respond to the start-up of the MISL?
The NASL started an indoor league in 1979, inviting its member teams to field indoor squads. Several did. In fact, during the NASL's last years, it had more teams competing in the indoor league than the outdoor league. Most definitely competition from the MISL hastened the demise of the NASL when fans turned to the faster action of indoor soccer. As the leagues vied for teams and the teams vied for players, costs escalated and media exposure fractured.

Prior to Major League Soccer, what was the most recent outdoor soccer league sanctioned by the United States Soccer Federation as outdoor professional?
In its bid to host the 1994 World Cup, the United States Soccer Federation agreed to initiate a top-level nationwide league in the U.S. At the time of the bid, 1988, the top outdoor leagues were the American Soccer League (primarily East Coat teams), and the Western Soccer

Alliance (Western U.S.). They merged into the American Professional Soccer League in 1990 and became the first USSF sanctioned professional outdoor league since the NASL. Several of the members of the U.S. Men's National Team that went to the 1990 World Cup played for APSL teams, but the league's unstable attendance and low corporate support showed its financial vulnerability. A good example was the New Mexico Chile's, which played their first game on Good Friday, which also was a Friday the 13th. The New Mexico team averaged 4,800 fans per game throughout the season but still lost more than $200,000 and closed before the season ended. The league was criticized by FIFA as unsatisfactory, prompting the USSF to outline plans for Major League Soccer.

What did the American Professional Soccer League change its name to after MLS started up?
As the 1994 World Cup approached and the United States Soccer Federation worked to launch a top-level outdoor league in the U.S., it stepped on the toes of the leagues that had been carrying the load. The USSF sanctioned the National Professional Soccer League as a professional indoor league and gave the United States Interregional Soccer League (USISL) Division III outdoor status. The APSL, renamed the A-League, was declared a Division II professional league. On top of all them all would be Major League Soccer.

During what year was the first MLS game played?
FIFA chose the United States to host the 1994 World Cup with the understanding that the USSF would have a top level outdoor league operating before the first World Cup game. USSF got an extension until 1995 and in 1995 announced another one-year delay. In 1996 Major League Soccer played its first game. Claudio Reyna celebrated the start of MLS, writing that the absence of a true professional

league had left college soccer "the top level of the game in the United States." As a result, college programs were the feeders of the national teams. To improve their skills post college, players were having to go abroad. Yet, only a few were talented enough to play abroad. Once MLS began, the best U.S. players had the opportunity to play for clubs in the U.S., giving more U.S. players the opportunity to improve their skills and providing a larger pool for the national team to choose from.

Of the 22 players from the U.S. Men's National Team that played in the 1994 World Cup, how many later joined MLS?
Of the 22, all but two later joined Major League Soccer. Fernando Clavijo, retired from playing immediately after the 1994 World Cup and spent some time coaching in MLS. Hugo Perez, retired after playing professionally in El Salvador.

Who was the first player to sign a contract with Major League Soccer?
He proved to the U.S. television audience how rough soccer can be when he took a bone-shattering elbow to the skull during the match between the United States and Brazil of the 1994 World Cup. On television 32 million people saw Tab Ramos convulsing on the ground. His notoriety—from that game, his play with the U.S. National Team, and his roots in New Jersey—made Ramos the perfect poster boy for the league when executives announced him as the first to sign with MLS.

How many years did the Women's United Soccer Association operate?
Launched in 2001, the league sought to take advantage of the wave of enthusiasm created by the 1999 Women's World Cup. Nevertheless, after the third season, league

administrators had to suspend operations because of
revenue shortfalls.

Major League Soccer

Who scored the first goal in Major League Soccer history?

Hosting D.C. United, the San Jose Clash nursed a scoreless
tie late into the second half on April 6, 1996. MLS
executives were sweating the idea that the league's first
game would validate the criticism that soccer did not offer
enough excitement for American fans. With two minutes
left Eric Wynalda knocked one in to give San Jose a 1-0
victory. The goal was later voted the goal of the year for
MLS.

Of the men who played in the outdoor North American Soccer League, how many also played in Major League Soccer?

The NASL played its final season in 1984, and MLS started
up in 1996. Only two players linked the two together.
Hugo Sanchez played for the San Diego Sockers in 1979
and 1980 before heading to Spain, Mexico, and Austria. He
came back to the U.S. and played for Dallas during the
1996 MLS season. Roy Wegerle played for the Tampa Bay
Rowdies in 1984 and the Tampa Bay Mutiny in 1998. His
other MLS teams were Colorado and D.C. Frank Klopas
came close to playing outdoor soccer in both leagues.
Going backward in time, he played in MLS for the Chicago
Fire in 1999 and 1998. Previously he played for Kansas
City, also in MLS, and in indoor leagues before MLS had
begun. One of those earlier campaigns was the NASL's
indoor league of 1984-1985. Klopas had signed with the
Chicago Sting, expecting to play in the NASL's outdoor
season, but a broken leg kept him sidelined until the indoor

season started up. When the outdoor season came around again, the NASL had folded.

Who writes the bulk of the rules for Major League Soccer?

Much earlier in this book was text about Great Britain's refusal to join FIFA. When the British countries did join, they did so under the condition that their own International Football Association Board would control the rules going forward. That body was composed of representatives from England, Wales, Northern Ireland, and Scotland. Since then the I.F.A.B. has added some representatives from FIFA and subtracted some representatives from FIFA and added some again. Today the I.F.A.B. is still FIFA's rule-making arm, and the whole world is expected to use those rules. To play with exceptions to those rules, leagues are required to get permission from FIFA.

Through 2006 how many World Cup Golden Boot winners have played in MLS?

During the 1994 World Cup, Hristo Stoitchkov won a share of the award for most goals, scoring six for Bulgaria. In 2000 he joined MLS's Chicago Fire, staying there for three seasons. For the 2003 season he played with D.C. united. He scored 22 goals in the regular season and another four goals in playoff games. No other golden boot winner has joined MLS teams.

During the 24 hours prior to the first Major League Soccer championship game, how many inches of rain did the Boston Area get?

It rained so much that a boat race was cancelled. In all it measured four inches.

What city had an original MLS team that was folded by the league after the 2001 season?

One of the marketing principles of the league has been the necessity of generating attention from the national media. Toward that goal, MLS founders chose the first team locations with geographic diversity in mind. One of those original teams was the Tampa Bay Mutiny. The balancing variable concerning geographic diversity was a team's attendance and local sponsorships. Tampa Bay fell short in both, leading the league to close down the Mutiny after the 2001 season.

What MLS team existed for the least amount of time?
The league expanded from 10 to 12 teams in 1998 by starting up the Chicago Fire and the Miami Fusion. With a league decision to cut back from 12 teams to 10, Miami and Tampa Bay were closed down after the 2001 season. For Miami it had been a life of only three seasons.

How old was Bobby Convey when he played for the first time in MLS?
On April 25, 2000, Convey started for D.C. United as a 16-year-old, then the youngest player to ever appear for an MLS team. He started 17 more games and appeared in four others that season. Since then he has played four more seasons with MLS, earned more than 30 caps for the U.S. Men's National Team, and transferred to play in England.

Through 2006, who is the only MLS player in a regular season game to play goalie and score a goal?
On July 5th, 2003, the MetroStars were in extra time and out of subs for field players. Since FIFA has long allowed goalkeepers and field players to switch at any stoppage of play, the MetroStars managed to squeeze in another sub. First they switched Tim Howard, who was in goal at the time, with a field player. Since MLS allowed an extra sub for goalkeepers, the MetroStars then subbed in Eddie Gaven to play in goal. Gaven then handed the gloves to

Howard, who was still a field player, and Gaven went out to play in the field. Gaven ended up scoring the game winner for his team a couple minutes later. The rule for an extra goalkeeper sub was later changed.

How many of its first 13 games in existence did the L.A. Galaxy win?

The Galaxy played its first game ever on April 13, 1996. More than 69,000 people attended the Galaxy's 2-1 win over the MetroStars. Los Angeles won two more games by the same, slim score and then beat D.C. United 3-1. Against San Jose the Galaxy won 2-1, followed by a 2-0 victory over Kansas City. Three straight one-goal victories drew even more attention as L.A. finished its ninth game with a 9-0 record. The Galaxy beat the MetroStars 4-0 for the 10th victory and then had to use a shootout for the 11th. By a 3-1 score L.A. beat Colorado at home on June 23 and then traveled to Denver to meet Colorado a week later. There and then, in the Galaxy's 13th game, the steak ended with a 2-1 loss. The 12 straight victories is still an MLS record.

For the 11 MLS seasons from 1996 through 2006 only one player played every season for the same team. Who?

He grew up in Southern California and then earned a spot on the UCLA team as a walk-on. Before the 1996 season Cobi Jones joined the L.A. Galaxy and has been there ever since.

Through 2006 what is the record for most consecutive seasons that one person has coached an MLS team?

He's a former coach of the U.S. Men's National team. In mid-season in 1999 Bob Gansler took over as the head coach of the Kansas City Wizards and stayed into the 2006 season.

Names, Mascots, and Jerseys

What was the hyped-up name of the championship game of the North American Soccer League?
At first it was simply the NASL Championship Game. In 1975, though, league executives dusted off the title that had applied to the college championship before the NCAA had created the post-season tournament. NASL's championship became known as the Soccer Bowl.

Who was the U.S. Open Cup Tournament trophy renamed in honor of in 1999?
The tournament has been around since 1914, almost as long as Lamar Hunt has been investing in professional soccer in the U.S. Likely nobody has spent so much money on soccer in the United States. Hunt, better known as the owner of the NFL's Kansas City Chiefs (and the man who coined the term *Super Bowl*), owned the NASL's Dallas Tornado, which was the league's longest operating franchise in one city, lasting from 1967 until 1981. When Major League Soccer began its organizational phase, Hunt was there again, becoming the lead investor in teams in Columbus and Kansas City. He later bought into MLS's team in Dallas and led the effort to build a soccer specific stadium for the Columbus Crew and F.C. Dallas. For all that effort, USSF put Hunt's name on the trophy awarded to the winner of the U.S. Open Cup.

What is the name of the championship trophy for Major League Soccer?
As chairman of the United States Soccer Federation and the 1994 World Cup, Alan Rothenberg had obligated himself to FIFA to start a national professional outdoor soccer league in the U.S. The result was Major League Soccer. As the founder, Rothenberg's name is on the trophy given to the league's champion.

What was the name of San Diego's soccer team that started in the NASL and moved into the MISL?
The San Diego Sockers were arguably the most successful professional team of all-time in the United States. After a transient life that started in 1974, the team settled in San Diego for the NASL's 1978 season. They made the NASL playoffs that year and in 1979, 1980, 1981, 1982, and 1984. Hungarian Julie Veee carried the team for much of that time, especially when it took up the indoor game. The Sockers won the NASL indoor title in 1982 while Veee scored at least two goals in each of the 17 games he played in that season. When the team moved to the Major Indoor Soccer League, San Diego won the league championship in 1983. Veee was the playoff MVP. Bouncing back to the NASL, the Sockers won the second NASL indoor championship, played in 1984.

Pele, Bob Rigby, Giorgio Chinaglia, and Bobby Moore played together for three games in 1976 in the U.S. What was that team called?
The NASL put together an all-star team plus three Americans that rivaled any other mess of players ever combined on the planet. They played in the Bicentennial Soccer Cup, a tournament against England, Italy, and Brazil. Team America, as the NASL stars were known, lost to Italy 4-0, Brazil 2-0, and England 3-1.

There was a later group involved with the NASL called Team America. What was that about?
The idea was to put together a team of U.S. players to reach higher levels of playing, coaching, and fitness for preparation toward the 1984 Olympics and 1986 World Cup. They played as a team in the NASL during the 1983 season under the name Team America.

What did Jim McAllister leave the field with after his last NASL game of the 1977 season?
McAllister, the rookie of the year for 1977, was part of the Seattle Sounders, the team that faced the New York Cosmos in the championship game. The Cosmos walked off the field with the trophy, but McAllister, took advantage of the traditional post-game swap and walked off the field with the last jersey ever worn by Pele in an NASL game.

Tatu played for the indoor Dallas Sidekicks. How did he celebrate scoring goals?
Playing in the Major Indoor Soccer League, Tatu scored 390 goals. He scored almost 300 more while Dallas was part of the Continental Indoor Soccer League and the World Indoor Soccer League. After many of those goals, Tatu would throw his jersey to somebody in the crowd.

After the 1990 World Cup game between the United States and Italy, what item of clothing did John Harkes exchange with Giuseppe Giannini?
As they walked through the tunnel that led to the dressing room after the game, Harkes exchanged jerseys with Italian Riccardo Ferri. Giannini, a bit too late on the traditional exchange, approached Harkes to trade but found that Harkes was already holding an Azzurri jersey. So Giannini pointed at his shorts, and the two shucked them on the spot and traded with each other.

A lot of people thought that Brandi Chastain's bra brandishing was staged. After all, prior to the 1999 Women's World Cup, she had posed fully naked for a magazine. What magazine?
Chastain's first notable pose came for Nike in an ad with her back bare. Then came a photo of a well-placed soccer ball in front of her full nakedness for *Gear Magazine*. It ran just prior to the start of the tournament.

Did any other players in the 1999 Women's World Cup go jersey-less in front of the cameras?
For weeks following the tournament, Chastain was asked during interviews if the jersey relief was staged. Her full explanation came in her book *It's Not about the Bra*. She says that there was no way that she could have had the foresight and the clear mind to have pulled it off, so to speak. Her explanation is quite believable for a couple other reasons, the last of which is that she had no idea until minutes prior that she could be the final kicker for the U.S. Men have often taken of their jerseys as part of goal celebrations, and they got beamed into households doing just that during the 1998 Men's World Cup. Anyone who had watched those games, including Chastain, would have seen the frequent displays. Also, as many of the men did in the same tournament and in games throughout the past decades, women players in 1999 began exchanging jerseys after their matches. When the women doffed their shirts, they showed bodies clad more heavily than some bodies in commercials that paid for the games. The taboo was being chipped away at during the tournament as women exchanged jerseys after games and lifted them off after goals. Chastain just let go and broke the barrier for good.

In February 2005 American Eddie Lewis was sent off in a game between his Preston North End team and QPR of England's second highest division. The referee sent somebody else to the stands that day. Who?
Lewis was guilty of play deemed too physical. Jude the Cat, QPR's mascot, was guilty of meowing in dissent. The referee, Lee Probert, sent the mascot to the stands after the mascot protested an offside call.

What was the name of the official mascot of the 1994 World Cup?
The appropriate name *Striker* was given to the cartoon dog

that walked on its hind legs wearing socks and soccer shoes. The inappropriate aspect of him was that when he first was unveiled he was holding the soccer ball and wearing a jersey that looked more like one from a rugby team. Modifications were made quickly to give Striker a more soccer-looking jersey and to give him the gravity-defying ability to keep the ball at his feet at all times.

What was the original name of MLS's San Jose team?
The team was called the Clash for four seasons. It then became the Earthquakes, using the name of the NASL team that had made the Bay Area home years earlier.

What was the original name of MLS's Kansas City team?
The team started operating under the name *The Wiz*, and met some, we'll call it legal throat-clearing, from the folks who run the music stores Nothing Beats the Wiz. After using the name for one season, the team announced a change for the 1997 season, going with Wizards.

What does Preki's last name begin with?
You will have to trust me on this because finding his last name is no simple task. Seriously, the guy goes by Preki. However, when you sign up to play in the World Cup, FIFA requires a passport, and his passport led FIFA to put him on the U.S. roster as Predrag Radosavljevic.

Coaches and Captains

Dick Advocaat has coached the national teams of Holland, United Arab Emirates, and South Korea. What team did he play for from 1978 through 1980?
Advocaat took Holland into the quarterfinals of the 1994 World Cup. He later coached the same nation to the

semifinals of Euro 2004, the national teams' tournament of
Europe. Long earlier, though, he was playing for the
Chicago Sting of the NASL.

**During the 1994 World Cup, Carlos Alberto Parreira
coached Brazil to the championship. Who was he
coaching in 1997?**
This team had three coaches during MLS's first calendar
year of play and through 2005 has had more coaches than
any other MLS team. Parreira came on when Carlos
Queiroz left at the end of 1996. He had replaced Eddie
Firmani, the first MetroStars coach. Parreira made way for
Alfonso Mondelo, who was replaced by Bora Milutinovic,
who was replaced by Fernando Clavijo on an interim basis,
giving way to Octavio Zambrano, who lasted almost two
years. When he got the boot in 2002, the team brought in
Bob Bradley, who lasted into 2005 to be replaced by Mo
Johnston.

**One of England's players during the team's loss to the
U.S. in 1950 was Alf Ramsey. He later went into
coaching. As a coach what was his highest
accomplishment?**
Ramsey played in all three of England's games in 1950,
including the 1-0 upset by the U.S. Years later he became
the coach of England's national team and took it to the
1966 World Cup, predicting a championship even though
England's World Cup record was three wins, six losses, and
five draws. He validated that prophesy by beating West
Germany in the final, and was knighted. To this day it is
the only World Cup championship for England.

**The Los Angeles Aztecs coach from 1978 until 1980 was
Rinus Michels. How high was his previous coaching
experience?**
Michels was the guy who created total football, the concept

that every player should be skillful and adaptable enough to be able to play any position on the field. He coached the Netherlands into the 1974 World Cup final and was named the coach of the century by FIFA in 1999. From 1978 until 1980, he coached the Los Angeles Aztecs, of the NASL. During 1979, he coached Dutch great Johan Cruyff, who played with the Aztecs for one season.

How many times did Tony DiCicco, the former head coach of the U.S. Women's National Team, play for the U.S. Men's National Team?
DiCicco, a goalkeeper, played for five years in the American Soccer League and appeared one time for the U.S. Men's National Team, in 1973.

Who coached the United States National Team during the 1994 Men's World Cup?
With so much attention on the United States during the 1994 tournament, the United States Soccer Federation wanted proven leadership and a spot in the second phase, the round of 16. Bora Milutinovic had coached Mexico into the World Cup's final eight in 1986 and Costa Rica into the round of 16 in 1990. After taking the U.S. team into the round of 16 in 1994, Milutinovic went on to coach Nigeria in the 1998 World Cup, reaching the round of 16, and China in the 2002 World Cup.

What player with the U.S. Men's National Team was named captain for life?
During a trip to England in early 1996, Coach Steve Sampson told John Harkes that Harkes would be the captain of the team. Although Sampson claims that he never gave out the title *ad vita*, he seems to have never corrected media reports that he had given that full honor. So came a comical spin on the situation when Sampson removed from the team his captain for life just two years

after naming him that and just two months prior to the 1998
World Cup. Making light of the episode, Harkes penned an
autobiography and titled it *Captain for Life—And Other
Temporary Assignments*.

Who was the captain of the United States Men's National team during the 1998 World Cup?

After dismissing John Harkes, Steve Sampson appointed a
new captain, Thomas Dooley, who had been born in
Germany and had played most of his professional soccer in
Germany.

How did the U.S. do against Iran during the 1998 World Cup?

The United States certainly was favored to win the game,
but the game proved to be an over-correction that led to a
slow-motion train wreck. Following his team's 2-0 loss to
Germany, U.S. Coach Steve Sampson dropped five starters
and reverted to a previous formation to face Iran. It would
have been a brilliant move had Iran not scored in the 40th
minute. After Sampson made three subs, Iran scored in the
84th minute. Brian McBride did pull one back for the U.S.,
but the game ended 2-1. Without hope of moving into the
second round, some U.S. players—the ones getting playing
time, the ones sitting on the bench, and the ones left at
home—publicly criticized Sampson for everything he had
done since birth. Sampson resigned before the end of the
tournament.

What happened to Steve Sampson?

He was shot.

Was Steve Sampson really shot?

For decades the coaches for the United States Men's
National Team were foreign born. Sampson, a U.S. citizen,
turned the tables. After leaving the helm of the U.S. Men's

National Team, he hung out in California before accepting the job as coach for the national team of Costa Rica. He led the team through several matches including two qualifiers for the 2006 World Cup. In all, his record for Costa Rica was 11-7 plus four ties.

After Steve Sampson gave up the job as coach of the U.S. Men's National Team, Bruce Arena took the job. The two had met in the 1989 NCAA Division I college championship game. What was the result of that contest between the two coaches?
Sampson's Santa Clara team went 20-0-3 that season while Arena's Virginia team went 21-2-2. After two overtimes in the championship game and a 1-1 score, that's where the game ended. Both teams shared the championship.

In all how many more titles did Steve Sampson and Bruce Arena win as college coaches?
Sampson never won another title. Arena took four championships in four consecutive years: 1991, 1992, 1993, and 1994.

Did Bruce Arena ever play professionally?
I could make this into a sophomoric, trick question by explaining that Arena did play professionally in 1975 with the Montreal Quebecois, a professional *lacrosse* league. However, a year later he played professional soccer with the Tacoma Tides, of the American Soccer League.

How many times has Coach Bruce Arena appeared as a player for the U.S. Men's National Team?
As a goalie Arena sat on the bench as the U.S. started a game against Israel on November 15, 1973. But he did come in before the end of the 2-0 loss, earning him his one and only cap.

Why wasn't Bruce Arena on the bench when the U.S. met Costa Rica and Barbados in World Cup qualifying in 2000?
During a World Cup qualifying match against Costa Rica in Costa Rica in 2000, referee Peter Prendergast called a crap penalty kick against the United States in stoppage time of the second half while the score was tied 1-1. Costa Rica scored, and the game ended 2-1. Captain Claudio Reyna argued with the referee after the call and after the game and threw his captain's band at the referee. Head Coach Bruce Arena also criticized the call on the field and after the game. Reyna and Arena each were given a two-game suspension, leaving Reyna off the field and Arena away from the bench during the home game against Costa Rica and a must-win game against Barbados. Five years later Arena again was ejected, during a Gold Cup semifinal match against Honduras. It, too, was dealt by referee Peter Prendergast.

During the 2004 MLS season, Sigi Schmidt was replaced as coach of the Los Angeles Galaxy. At the time he was fired, what place was Schmidt's team among the five teams in MLS's Western Conference?
Schmidt's team had more points than any other in the league and was at the top of the conference when he was fired. Team management cited the fact that the Galaxy had been winless in its previous five games.

Who replaced Schmidt as Galaxy coach in 2004?
After Steve Sampson fell out of any spotlight, he managed to get a job coaching the Costa Rica National Team, only to get fired in 2004. Available, he was named by Galaxy management to replace Schmidt two days after Schmidt was booted into the stands. The team's record when he took the reigns was 9-6-7. Under Sampson the team won two, lost three and tied three, made it to the playoffs, and

lost in the conference final. The next season he led the team to its second championship.

Who was the U.S. National Women's Team player who captained the team through the 1991 World Cup and later became the team's coach?

Thinking that she was destined for a career coaching basketball, April Heinrichs headed to a Colorado college after high school on a basketball scholarship. Before the end of her freshmen year, she got in contact with Anson Dorrance, the head soccer coach for the women's program at the University of North Carolina. She transferred there, won three national college championships, and made her way onto the women's national team. In 1991 she was the captain of the team. She became an assistant coach of the women's national team and then the head coach in 2000, leading the team to the 2004 Olympic gold medal.

What former Chicago Sting player (NASL) went on to coach the U.S. Women's National Team?

Greg Ryan. He played six seasons in the NASL, including 1981, when the Sting won the Soccer Bowl.

Who was the first coach to put Chris Armas on the field for the U.S. Men's National Team?

Easily the MVP for MLS Cup '98 could have been Chris Armas for his defending on Marco Etcheverry. Ty Keough called Etcheverry "the best playmaker on these two teams" and then gave Armas credit for shutting him down. At that time, Armas had yet to play for the U.S. Men's National Team and was playing in front of Bruce Arena, Etcheverry's coach. That game was Arena's last as coach of D.C. United before he accepted the head coaching spot for the men's national team. Two weeks later when Arena made his debut with the U.S. Men's National Team, he had Armas on his team and put him on the field in the 46th minute.

What U.S. player was named to the 2002 World Cup all-star team?
As a midfielder who played in four of the U.S.'s games and was the captain of the team, Claudio Reyna earned his way onto the all-star team. He was the only person from the three CONCACAF teams who was given the honor.

Who has the most coaching wins with professional soccer teams in the United States?
After playing professionally in England, Ron Newman came to the U.S. to play and then coach. He first coached Lamar Hunt's Dallas Tornado in the NASL and won the league's outdoor championship in 1971. He coached other NASL teams during outdoor seasons and teams in the indoor NASL, American Soccer League, Major Indoor Soccer League, and Continental Indoor Soccer League. He won a total of 13 titles before rejoining Hunt to coach Kansas City of Major League Soccer in 1996. When he retired in 1999, Newman's professional record for indoor, outdoor, regular season, and playoffs was 753-296-27. No other professional coach in the U.S. has as many as 500 victories.

Mr. President

Which U.S. presidential election featured the first use of the demographic designation *soccer mom*?
The term was introduced in 1982 in a periodical in Ludlow, Massachusetts, and appeared only sporadically until the 1996 election. Alex Castellanos, a Republican consultant, told the *Wall Street Journal,* "The working soccer mom is the swing vote of this election."

Who was the last chairman of the board of the North American Soccer League?

He encouraged FIFA to play the 1986 World Cup in the
U.S. and tried again—successfully—for the 1994 World
Cup. Henry Kissinger helped bring Pele to the NASL and
regularly dropped into locker rooms after NASL games. By
serving as the top man for the league, he gave it some
legitimacy at a time when legitimacy was slipping away
quickly.

**What caused the United States Olympic Soccer Team to
miss the 1980 games?**
The United States Olympic Team earned a spot in the
Olympics by going 4-1-1 against Costa Rica, Bermuda and
Suriname. It was only the second time since 1956 that the
U.S. had qualified for the tournament. However, President
Jimmy Carter's decision to boycott the games kept the team
home.

**On November 19, 1987, somebody important hosted
FIFA President Jao Havelange in Washington D.C. and
asked him to choose the U.S. as host for the 1994 World
Cup. Who?**
The meeting took place in the Oval Office of the White
House with USSF President Warner Fricker and President
Ronald Reagan. Reagan made the pitch, leaving Havelange
to talk about how impressed he had been with the U.S.'s
effort for the Olympics three years earlier.

**Who played for Phillips Academy's varsity soccer team
from 1939 through 1941 and was its captain in 1941?**
The prestigious Massachusetts prep school also is known as
Andover. Its list of alumnae includes George Bush, class of
1942. During his days at the school, Bush played
basketball, baseball, and soccer, and during the 1941 season
he was the soccer team's captain. Soon after leaving the
school, he entered the military to fight in World War II.

What soccer-related reason did U.S. Women's National Team player Catherine Reddick give for preferring George W. Bush to Bill Clinton?
Reddick played for the University of North Carolina from 2000 through 2004. During her freshman year, UNC took the NCAA title but was not invited to the White House by President Clinton for a congratulatory photo and handshake. When Reddick and her teammates won again, in 2003, they were invited the White House by the new president, George W. Bush.

What gift did Captain Julie Foudy bring to the White House after she led her team to the 1999 Women's World Cup title?
President Bill Clinton was still getting over the scandal of Monica Lewinsky and impeachment when he figuratively and literally embraced the women's national team. He and his family appeared at games, commented about the team's on-going success, and invited them to the White House after the tournament. Once in the White House, Foudy, handed a cigar to a teammate and said, "The president wanted me to give you this." For further explanation of cigars in the Clinton White House, readers need to refer to a book other than this one.

Goalkeepers

Who played goalkeeper for the U.S. during the 1950 World Cup?
As a former professional baseball player, Frank Borghi joined St. Louis's Simpkins-Ford S.C. and became known for throwing the ball past half field. He helped his team win the 1948 National Open Cup and then joined the U.S. National Team that went to Brazil for the 1950 World Cup. There, Borghi shut out England's national team for one of

the biggest upsets in World Cup history. Borghi was following in the foot steps of Pete Renzulli, who picked up soccer only when his baseball team was meeting in the same park that a soccer game was being played. At the time, 1910, Renzulli was a minor league shortstop living in the Bronx. Told not to kick the ball with his baseball cleats, he stepped in goal and proved to be pretty good. He joined the team as the only American born player in the New York State Football Association, eventually won three open cup titles, and was inducted into the U.S. Soccer Hall Fame with the first class.

The two goalkeepers who played for the U.S. during the 1972 Olympics were Mike Ivanow and Shep Messing. They crossed paths a couple more times, most notably when the 1977 NASL championship came about. What did the future hold for Ivanow?

During that championship game, Ivanow sat the bench for Seattle as Messing played in goal for New York. Like many players in the NASL, Ivanow worked a second job. Having parents with roots in Russia, he worked at the Russian-American Credit Union in San Francisco until he was convicted of embezzling $70,000. While he sat on the bench of the championship game of 1977, he was preparing to serve three years in prison.

In 1983 goalkeeper Tino Lettieri was the NASL North American Player of the Year. What toy did he keep near his goal during games?

Lettieri, more than most goalkeepers, was a little eccentric. He kept Ozzie, a stuffed parrot, nearby during games. Ozzie, a replica of one of Lettieri's real birds, became a merchandising giant as Lettieri moved among NASL teams and played for Canada's Olympic and national team squads. Lettieri was seen kissing Ozzie before saving a penalty kick and talking to the bird during games. One version of Ozzie

lost an eye on a wide shot and another was stolen by fans.
While Lettieri was playing for the Vancouver Whitecaps in
1983, replicas of the replica were second only to Cabbage
Patch Dolls in toy sales there during the Christmas season.
However, the bird was not always a benefit to Lettieri. The
goalkeeper, while playing for the Minnesota Strikers, once
earned a caution for talking to Ozzie too long before a PK.
Later in the same game, Lettieri displayed a different type
of bird, earning his second caution and an exit from the
game. His team lost that game in overtime.

**Through 2006, which of these goalkeepers has the most
MLS championships: Kasey Keller, Brad Friedel, Tony
Meola, or Tim Howard?**
Among the four, only Meola has played in an MLS Cup.
He managed a shut out for the Kansas City Wizards in
2000, winning 1-0 over the Chicago Fire.

**What were goalkeeper Tony Meola's non-soccer athletic
goals following the 1994 World Cup?**
Meola, with his New Jersey accent and spider-web jersey,
got a lot of media exposure during the 1994 World Cup.
Without a top-level professional soccer league in the United
States at the time, though, he was thinking outside the box
for his future. He wanted to be an NFL kicker. He actually
signed a one-year contract with the New York Jets but
ended up playing soccer for the Long Island Roughriders
instead. When Major League Soccer got underway in 1996,
Meola was with the New York/New Jersey MetroStars.

**Who shared goalkeeping duties with Brianna Scurry for
the United States Women's National Team during the
1995 Women's World Cup game against Denmark?**
Scurry started the game but did not finish. Ahead 2-0
against Denmark, the United States was anticipating victory
with just a few minutes to play. With an eye on the next

match, the coaches used the last allowed substitution, but then Scurry got sent off. Assistant Coach April Heinrichs called Mia Hamm over to the touchline and informed her that her playful, post-practice goalkeeping had earned her the spot in goal. Hamm questioned the decision until she realized that the new goalkeeper would have to be one of the players on the field. Hamm put on the unique jersey and two gloves to face an immediate free kick from Denmark. The shot sailed high. She later made a save on a low cross before the game ended 2-0.

Did Michelle Akers score one of the penalty kicks for the United States Women's National Team during the tie-breaker of the championship game of the 1999 Women's World Cup?

Akers scored many penalty kicks for the women's national team, including one just days earlier during the semifinal against Brazil. By several accounts she had one of the hardest shots of any woman. She still reigns as the highest goal scorer in World Cup games. However, by the time the penalty-kick ticbreaker came about in that breathtaking match, Akers was in the dressing room hooked up to an intravenous tube. Suffering from Chronic Fatigue Syndrome, she had a hell of a time playing through the heat of that summer's six games. Just before the second half of the final ended, Akers collided with her goalkeeper, Brianna Scurry. Akers was dizzy and had difficulty standing up. When Head Coach Tony DiCicco asked her if she could go back in for the extra time, Akers said she could. Doug Brown, one of the team's doctors, told DiCicco otherwise and took Akers to the dressing room. From a medical table with a nearby television, Akers watched her teammates claim the title, and then walked with assistance out to the field to enjoy the crowd and accept her medal.

After leading her team to the gold medal of the 1996 Olympic Games, goalkeeper Briana Scurry made good on a promise. What was that promise?

Scurry, half-awake when interviewed, told a *Sports Illustrated* reporter that she would run naked through the streets of Georgia if the United States Women's National Team won the tournament. Weeks later and just prior to the championship game, *SI* printed her promise. Hours after the U.S. defeated China 2-1, Scurry donned her gold medal but nothing else to sprint a few yards through Athens, Georgia.

Who played 'keeper for the U.S. Women in the 2000 summer Olympics?

Brianna Scurry contributed to the U.S. women's gold medal of the 1996 Olympic Games and the championship of the 1999 Women's World Cup. When the 2000 Olympics came around, she was still suffering the affects of a pulled quad muscle, a stress fracture, and some weight gain. Siri Mullinix took the net and helped the team win the silver medal. Behind Scurry, Mullinex is the second most capped goalkeeper for the U.S. Women's National Team.

Friends and Family

Why did the members of the U.S. Men's National Team who played the final two qualifying games of the 1958 World Cup know each other so well?

St. Louis's Kutis team won the 1957 National Challenge Cup and the 1957 National Amateur Cup. Looking for an alternative to forming an all-star team of men unfamiliar with each other, the United States Soccer Federation decided to send the Kutis team to play Canada in two qualifying games.

During the 1994 World Cup, Bulgaria advanced into the round of 16 to face Mexico. The Bulgarian coach, however, was concerned about another group of people more than he was concerned about Mexico's team. What group of people was that?

Prior to 1994 Bulgaria had never won a game in a World Cup. After beating Greece and Argentina, earning a spot in the second phase, several of the Bulgarian players celebrated in Dallas. Some were captured in newspaper pictures while celebrating with women. Those photos made their way into Bulgarian newspapers and incited the players' wives to travel to the U.S. Anticipating the wives' arrival, Bulgaria's coach, Dimitar Penev, said that he "was more worried about what the wives would do to us" than he was worried about the next game.

For the 1990 World Cup, the roster of the U.S. team listed three players from the same city. Which city?

Kearny, New Jersey, was a working-class, immigrant city with a huge tradition in soccer. While so much of New Jersey and the rest of the country were being coached by people reading about soccer out of manuals, the Kearny boys were following fathers who had played and continued to play. The Kearny boys included Tony Meola, Tab Ramos, and John Harkes.

Which members of the U.S. Men's National Team played together during the 2002 World Cup and as 12-year-olds?

As youngsters, Claudio Reyna and Gregg Berhalter played for Union County, which was part of the Newark Sports Club. When they reached high school, they played at St. Benedict's, and were joined by Tab Ramos.

What married couple has seven NCAA Division I soccer titles from their college playing days?

If a single male were looking for a single female with Division I soccer championships, the sensible place to look would be the University of North Carolina. The sensible place to look for a male with championships in the middle 1990s would be the University of Virginia. That is the combination of Claudio Reyna and his wife, Danielle Egan. She played four years at North Carolina, winning four titles. He won three with UVa., leaving before his senior season.

What was Nicolette Richards' role with the U.S. Women's National Team during the 1999 Women's World Cup?
Richards' job was nanny for the three children that belonged to Carla Overbeck and Joy Fawcett. Fawcett's regular babysitter, Shannon MacMillan, was busy training with the team. Of course, the babysitters could not keep Overbeck and Fawcett on the field throughout their pregnancies. Overbeck once said that during the last months of pregnancy she would watch new players from the sidelines and would question her own heart and skills. She wondered, What if I can't get it back?

What U.S. Women's National Team player once quit a team that was coached by the person she would later marry?
University of Santa Clara Women's Soccer Coach Jerry Smith once called his best player into his office to tell her that he was unhappy with her attitude during her first year at the school. Brandi Chastain responded by quitting the team. Two days later Chastain reconsidered and talked to Smith. She acknowledged that she had been "mouthy, disrespectful and lazy in practice". Smith is no slouch as far as a coach. Since taking over the team in 1987, he has led it to the 2001 NCAA Division I title and more than 300 victories. The two have been married since 1996.

How does Julie Foudy keep up with her coach from her days as an under-19 club player?
She married him. She and Ian Sawyers were married in 1995.

As members of the national team player pool going into the 1999 Women's World Cup, Tracy Ducar and Debbie Keller were teammates. What was their legal connection to each other?
A year prior to the 1999 Women's World Cup, Keller filed a civil suit alleging that the head coach at the University of North Carolina had made romantic advances toward her while she was playing for him. Keller's suit also named the assistant coach, Tracy Ducar, for her role in the atmosphere of the team. Working toward the World Cup, the two found themselves as teammates at the same time that they were opposing litigants. Ducar made the final roster; Keller did not. Keller also lost the suit.

Eric Biefeld has two caps for the United States. Who's his better-known sister who happens to have a history with the U.S. Women's National Team?
After winning an NCAA championship in 1985 with the UCLA Bruins, Eric Biefeld made those two national team appearances. A year after his debut, his sister, Joy, was called up to play for the women's national team. In 1991 she married and changed her last name to Fawcett, which is how she is more commonly listed on the rosters of the 200-plus games she appeared in. Joy partially credits her brother for getting her interested in soccer when she was younger, and she considers him one of her idols.

One of the New York Cosmos' last contracted players was Andranik Eskandarian. What's his son's name?
Andranik Eskandarian played for Iran during the 1978 World Cup before joining the New York Cosmos in 1979.

There he stayed until the team's last days in 1984. His son, Alecko, grew up with the game in New Jersey and went on to play in college for the University of Virginia. In 2002 he won the M.A.C. Hermann Trophy, recognizing him as the best male soccer player in Division I. He was the first overall draft pick of 2003 for D.C. United. In MLS Cup 2004, he scored twice and was named game MVP.

During the 2003 MLS season, Mike Nugent, of the MetroStars, held an informal volunteer job as a chauffeur. Who was his regular passenger?
Nugent was a New Jersey product who happened to live near Eddie Gaven. Gaven, at 17-years-old, earned a spot with the MetroStars that year. Without a diver's license, Gaven relied on his mother for his first two days as part of the team. She drove him to practice in the family's green mini-van and picked him up afterward. Then Nugent offered to help. "I'm the chauffeur for Eddie," Nugent told the Newark *Star-Ledger*.

Why did Laura Cianciola, of Memphis, Tennessee, have to move her November 2003 wedding up by a couple months?
Cianciola is a cousin of Ross Paule, who was playing for the MetroStars in 2002. Clint Mathis, playing for the MetroStars at the same time, hosted a party in August where MetroStars goalie Tim Howard met Cianciola. They dated, and he asked her in April 2003 to marry him. They picked a date, November 29, and worked out all the plans as Howard's MetroStars played into the meat of the 2003 MLS season. Then Manchester United signed Howard, and their world turned upside down. They exchanged the big production for an impromptu ceremony in New York's Central Park before heading for England.

Part-timers

Why didn't Ben McLaughlin go to the 1950 World Cup as a member of the U.S. Men's National Team?
McLaughlin, of the Philadelphia Nationals, had helped the United States finish second in the North American Championships, earning a spot in the World Cup in Brazil. However, McLaughlin never traveled to Brazil because he could not get time off from work.

When the New Bedford Whalers won a spot in the national championship game in 1932 it played without its goalkeeper Johnny Reder. Why?
Reder left the Whalers for a try-out with the Boston Red Sox and made his Major League debut on April 16 that year. In terms of successful teams, however, it proved to be the wrong directions for Reder. He played in a total of 17 major league games in his career. Meanwhile, his whalers won the national championship that year without him.

When the Ben Miller team played for the national title in 1926, why did it leave Jimmy Dunn behind in St. Louis?
Dunn had to stay in St. Louis to work. At the store he worked in, Dunn's manager would not give him permission to make the trip. At the time, Dunn had two children and did not want to risk his job by disobeying his boss. Without him, his team ended up losing 7-2 to Bethlehem Steel at Ebbets Field.

Why did goal-scorer Randy Horton practice so rarely for the Washington Diplomats in 1975?
When Horton came into the NASL in 1971, he won rookie of the year. In 1972 he was named league MVP. Obviously the guy was good. So when he needed weekdays off, the team was willing to be flexible. The reason that Horton

needed to miss practices was that he was an administrator
of a school in Bermuda.

When Shep Messing graduated from high school, what was his goal?

Messing pretty much quit playing soccer as he headed off
for Harvard University. He had been a stellar goalkeeper
during high school, was pretty good at track and field, and
was a .700 hitter for his Babe Ruth Baseball team. He had
a try-out with the Mets, and he was offered a pole vaulting
scholarship. During his college days at Harvard, he picked
up soccer again, later made the U.S. Olympic Team, and
eventually played in the NASL. His objective for college,
though, was to graduate with good enough grades to get
into law school.

After playing for the U.S. in the 1934 World Cup, what professional league did Buff Donelli coach in?

Donelli returned home from the 1934 World Cup and
continued playing club soccer. He also coached college
football teams and made his way to the top coaching job
with the Pittsburgh Steelers in 1942. He later coached with
the NFL's Cleveland Rams in 1944. After serving in World
War II, Donelli coached Columbia University's football
team for 11 years.

During the NFL's 1969 season, Momcilo Gavric played a couple games for the San Francisco 49ers as a kicker. He came back to the area in 1974 to play for another professional team. Which one?

In perhaps the only time in which a professional American
football player went on to make it on the soccer field,
Gavric played for the North American Soccer League's San
Jose Earthquakes from 1974 until 1976. During his 1969
NFL experience, he played in seven games and was 22 for
24 in extra points. It's fortunate for his team that it scored

so many touchdowns because Gavric was not as successful with field goals. There he made only 3 of 11.

In 1988 Lothar Osiander was waiting tables at Graziano's, a swanky restaurant in San Francisco's financial district. What was his soccer-related vocation?
Osiander was the coach of the United States Men's Olympic Team. He missed little work during the Olympics since the U.S. tied twice and lost, not good enough to advance to the knock-out phase.

After growing up in St. Louis playing soccer and baseball, Joe Garagiola played baseball for the Cardinals, Pirates, Cubs, and Giants. As part of a radio and television career that followed, he worked for the Cardinals, as a host of the NBC *Today Show,* and on weekly broadcasts of *The Game of the Week.* Along the way he also worked for the Yankees, where he met up with a childhood friend that had been a teammate of his on a youth soccer team in St. Louis. Both of them are in the Baseball Hall of Fame. Who's that long-time friend of Garagiola?
When Garagiola played soccer for the St. Ambrose School, the team won the parochial school championship, and Garagiola won his first medal of any kind. As part of another team, the Stags, Garagiola played with a guy who had strong legs, strong enough to squat through a 19-year career primarily as a catcher, earning three MVP awards and ten World Series rings. It's Yogi Berra.

Who's this? He grew up in Pennsylvania and served in World War II. While a member of the Philadelphia Nationals, he was chosen an all-star of the American Soccer League to play Liverpool F.C. during their 1946

**tour. After leaving pro soccer, he joined the FBI and
later started a security company.**
The American Soccer League was the league that provided
several players for the U.S. Men's National Team for
decades. It was also the league that included George
Wackenhut, who started The Wackenhut Corporation in
1954 and led it to become a security firm with clients on six
continents. He also served on the board of the U.S. Soccer
Hall of Fame.

**During the earliest years of the 20th Century, St. Leo's,
of St. Louis, won ten consecutive city championships,
the first St. Louis/Chicago championship, and a handful
of games against East Coast teams. John Tully and Bill
Abstein played for St. Leo's but also made news for
other professions. What were those other professions?**
Tully, a federal agent, went undercover as a Leavenworth
prisoner to break up a drug ring. Abstein played first base
for the Pittsburgh Pirates and won the World Series with
them in 1909, the season he hit .260.

**Who replaced Michelle Akers in the 1999 Women's
World Cup Final?**
After 90 minutes of scoreless play, Akers had to leave.
Head Coach Tony DiCicco and assistant Lauren Gregg
discussed her replacement and made an improbable
decision, 23-year-old Sara Whalen. Whalen had come into
the tournament with 33 previous appearances for the team,
compared to Akers' 141, and was just nine years old when
Akers played her first game for the women's national team.
Also, Whalen had been the last player chosen for the World
Cup roster.

**During the United States' game against Germany in the
1999 Women's World Cup, what did Shannon**

MacMillan do when she entered the game as a substitute?

When MacMillan came on the score was tied at two. She subbed in just in time to take a corner kick, one of her specialties for the team. Her line drive found Joy Fawcett at the near post. Fawcett headed the ball into the net for the winning goal and an assist for MacMillan on her first touch of the game.

Who sang the national anthem prior to MLS Cup 96?

Not involved in playing that day, Alexi Lalas lent his voice to the first ever championship game of Major League Soccer. Lalas was no Karaoke comic. He had been in a band for many years.

Injuries

What injury precipitated Gordon Banks' decision to come to the NASL?

Banks played goalkeeper for England during the 1966 World Cup, shutting out the team's first four opponents en route to claiming the trophy. After a 1972 auto accident, he was forced into coaching but returned to playing by joining the Ft. Lauderdale Strikers for their 1977 season. With a 37-year-old body and a lingering injury from the crash, Banks played every minute of the season, finishing with nine shutouts, and earning the league's MVP award. The team made it into the playoffs to face the New York Cosmos in a two-game playoff. Ft. Lauderdale lost the first match 8-3. When the teams met again, they finished 90 minutes of play tied 2-2. In the tie-breaker, Banks allowed the Cosmos to go up 1-0. Shep Messing, the Cosmos' goalie, made a save, keeping the score 1-0. Banks let in the second, and Messing made another save to put the score 2-0. The shootout then had to be stopped when Pele came running onto the field to celebrate the Cosmos' victory and embrace Messing. Messing explained to Pele that Ft. Lauderdale still had a chance. Banks then stopped a shot, as did Messing. The next Cosmos' shooter scored, ending the Strikers' season. The lingering injury that Banks dealt with was no sight in one eye.

How many years elapsed between Kate Sobrero Markgraf's first practice with the U.S. Women's National Team and her first appearance with the team in a game?
In 1995 Markgraf, after her freshman season at Notre Dame, was invited to try out with the U.S. Women's National Team. She was slightly ill and more than slightly out of shape, causing her to pass out during the first day of training. She left the camp without making the team and without the confidence she had arrived with. Still suffering emotionally from the failure, Markgraf quit the Notre Dame team during her sophomore season. Her parents pushed her to return, and she did a week later. Her Notre Dame team made its way into the NCAA tournament and into the championship game. With Markgraf earning defensive MVP honors for the tournament, Notre Dame took home the title. U.S. Coach Tony DiCicco called her again, but she declined to return to the national team camp. In fact, she kept declining for another two years. In January 1998 she gave in. During one of the training sessions, Markgraf collided with another player, breaking her own jaw and losing a tooth. She recovered to make an appearance for the team three months later, three years after her first training session.

Who's this? She failed out of college once, tore both ACLs, tore an MCL during an Olympic semifinal, was kicked off a college team, and failed to make the

national team prior to the 1995 World Cup before coming back to earn more than 150 caps?
The question would be too simple if it had asked who scored the penalty kick that won the 1999 Women's World Cup for the U.S. The person is Brandi Chastain. After that penalty kick she was named one of People magazine's 25 most intriguing people of the year, reached 97th in Street and Smith's most powerful people in sports, and threw out the first pitch in a New York Yankees game.

Who's this? She missed out on her first chance to join the U.S. Women's National Team when mononucleosis hit her. She later made the team but was cut from the 1996 squad before the Olympic Games in Atlanta. The very coaches she bemoaned then called her back before the Olympics started to give her another chance. She scored three goals in the Atlanta games, including the overtime golden goal against Norway that put the United States into the final.
When she was young Shannon MacMillan told friends that she was going to play soccer in the Olympics even though that was at least five years before the Olympics included women's soccer and a couple years before mono knocked her out of the tryout. During the 1996 games, she also scored the game-winner against Sweden. In 2002 she was named the U.S. Soccer's Chevrolet Female Athlete of the Year.

What was the scheduling problem between Michelle Akers and the games of the 1999 Women's World Cup?
Two of the games were scheduled past her bed time. Akers, who suffered from severe chronic fatigue syndrome, usually went to bed around 8:30. And it was not just sleepiness; her body was shutting down. Using caffeine and social stimulation, team trainers began changing Akers' body clock three months before the tournament started.

What caused Michelle Akers to nearly miss the 1991 Women's World Cup?
Three months before the first game of the first women's world championship, Akers slid over a sprinkler head during practice, cutting open her leg. Doctors gave her 35 stitches and cautioned her that another collision could open up her leg again. She played anyway, scoring 10 goals in six games, including two against Norway in the 2-1 final.

During the 1999 Women's World Cup the U.S. played North Korea in the third game of the first round. How many minutes did Michelle Akers play before getting injured?
With the likelihood that the U.S. women could qualify for the next round without her, Akers sat out the entire game. After a 3-0 win assured them of moving into the round of eight, the entire U.S. team took a jog around Foxboro Stadium to high-five the fans. One fan grabbed Akers' hand as she ran by, causing her a slight shoulder dislocation and the need for regular ice packs throughout the rest of the tournament. When she re-injured the same shoulder later, she decided to call it a career.

Who's this? He was born in New York City and played five games for Puerto Rico. After a battle with FIFA, he was given permission to play with the U.S. Men's National Team on November 5, 1998. The next day he earned his first U.S. cap. He made the U.S. Olympic team in 2000 but was taken off the roster when he suffered a knee injury prior to the tournament. After earning 45 caps he made the roster for the 2002 World Cup. However, he tore his ACL a month before the tournament and was replaced.
He also was U.S. Soccer's Chevrolet Male Athlete of the Year for 2000. Chris Armas. Before falling victim to the

ACL tear that kept him out of the 2002 World Cup, Armas played in 14 of the 16 qualifiers.

Who's this? Like Chris Armas, he had to miss the 2000 Olympics because of a knee injury. When Armas got knocked out of the 2002 World Cup, this guy was called up as a last-second replacement.
As of May 2002 Armas and this guy had experienced heartbreak three times due to knee injuries. Then this guy, Steve Cherundolo, got to South Korea to replace Armas. There, Cherundolo injured a knee and was unable to play in any games.

Extra Time

In terms of overtime periods, what's the longest high school soccer game ever played in the U.S.?
When Farm Academy of Bristol, Ohio, played Erie High School, also of Ohio, on October 23rd, 1933, the game did not end for nine hours. Farm Academy won 1-0 after 28 extra periods.

What was used to decide tie games in the National Amateur Cup in 1950?
After playing to a 2-2 tie and a 1-1 tie against the Morgans, Harmarville moved past the Western Pennsylvania playoffs to the next round of the National Amateur Cup because the team had earned a greater number of corner kicks during the two matches. Even though this tie-breaker seems quite odd today, there is a story—more likely a hypothetical situation—of a soccer referee who put the advantage clause to use in a tie game that took into account corner-kicks. With just seconds left in the tie match, the referee watched a break-away for one team. The attacking player was brought down in the penalty area, allowing a defender to

clear the ball for a corner kick. The attacker certainly
deserved a penalty kick. However, thinking quickly, the
referee realized that the teams were tied on corner kicks as
well. The referee, knowing that penalty kicks are not
automatic goals, let the foul go. Instead he used the
advantage clause and awarded the attacking team a corner
kick, and thus the game.

**Which college is this? In 1981 its men's team reached
the Division I NCAA championship game by beating
Duke 1-0 in overtime, Clemson 3-1 in triple overtime,
West Virginia 2-1 in overtime, and Philadelphia 3-2 on
PKs.**
With those four cardiac victories, Alabama A&M reached
its first and only NCAA championship game in 1981.
There they lost to Connecticut 2-1 . . . in overtime.

**What percentage of MLS games ended in ties during
the league's first season?**
Out of concern for the notion the Americans don't
appreciate games absent a winner, Major League Soccer
initially required that teams duke it out until a team could
duke no longer. There were no ties. For the league's first
four years, games often ended in shoot-outs involving five
players from each team taking one-on-ones. Soccer purists,
often the most annoying people in the stands, paid young
kids to hold up signs demanding, "ban the shootout". Such
displays encouraged MLS to change its rules and let ties
stand beginning with the fifth season.

**What innovation did FIFA first use to decide tie games
during the knock-out round of the 1998 World Cup?**
Tie games used to bring about do-overs, or replays. That
created scheduling problems as the World Cup added
television and more teams. Extra time was extended and
then penalty kicks were used in the 1982 World Cup for the

first time. The 1994 World Cup brought heaping criticism about penalty-kick tie-breakers, mostly because the final was decided on PKs. Also in 1994 More than one coach admitted to playing defensively with an interest in reaching penalty kicks. Seeing the opportunity to reduce the number of games reaching PKs, FIFA added the golden goal to the 1998 World Cup. The first team to score in extra time would be declared the winner—no chance for the other team to tie it up again and take a game to PKs.

For the first time ever in a World Cup final, the 1994 champion was decided by penalty kicks. Something else unique happened in the 1994 World Cup involving the penalty-kick tie-breaker when Romania and Sweden met. What was it?

The penalty-kick tie-breaker was used in the World Cup for the first time in 1982. Some classic games have gone to that point, always inviting criticism about the best-of-five roll of the dice. The best-of-five went further in 1994, though, when the shootout moved into sudden death for the first time ever in a World Cup. Romania and Sweden, playing in Stanford Stadium, each scored four of their first five. On the team's sixth shot, Sweden scored and then its goalkeeper, Thomas Ravelli, saved a shot from Romania, giving Sweden a 5-4 margin on PKs, thus a 3-2 victory in the game.

Did Italy's Roberto Baggio score a penalty kick in the 1994 World Cup?

Italy was the worst team to make the second phase of the World Cup that was played in the U.S. With four points, it was a third place team in group play. Following his tying goal in the 88th minute against Nigeria, Baggio won the team's first game of the knock-out round with a successful PK in extra time. In the next game he scored in the 87th minute to beat Spain. In the semifinals he scored both of

Italy's goals to beat Bulgaria. Regardless of those five goals to carry his team to the championship match, Roberto Baggio is remembered for the goal he missed. After a scoreless 90 minutes and extra time, the final match was decided on PKs. Needing to score to keep Italy alive, Baggio sent his PK into the stands, giving the title to Brazil.

After being told that she was to take one of the penalty kicks at the end of the final game of the 1999 Women's World Cup, what did Mia Hamm suggest?
Hamm, the scorer of more international goals than any other man or woman, often suffered a lack of confidence. Anxious about being one of the five U.S. shooters, she was confused when she heard the list of shooters read to the players just prior to the PKs starting. Hamm turned to ask Shannon MacMillan where in the order MacMillan would be shooting. MacMillan answered that she was not on the list to take a shot. Hamm asked her, "Do you want one?" And MacMillan replied, "Yeah, sure." So Hamm went to Assistant Coach Lauren Gregg, suggesting she be replaced by MacMillan. Gregg told Hamm that Hamm could not back out because the list had already been given to the referees. Hamm took the team's fourth shot and scored.

After the 1999 Women's World Cup, what three experiences had FIFA believing that playing major games in the Rose Bowl was a bad idea?
Brazil won the 1994 Men's World Cup when Italy's Roberto Baggio sent his penalty kick into the seats of the Rose Bowl, ending the tie-breaker and a scoreless final. Five years later the Women's World Cup played the third place game and the final in the Rose Bowl. Each of those scoreless games needed a penalty-kick shootout as well. When FIFA decided to play the 2003 Women's World Cup in the United States, organizers scheduled the final in the Home Depot Center, across town from the Rose Bowl.

Caps

How many qualifying games does a player have to appear in to be eligible for a national team's roster for the World Cup?
While trying to win qualifying games, coaches also use the matches to evaluate players in his effort to pick a team for the World Cup. Regardless, coaches may choose players for the World Cup team who have not appeared at all in qualifiers. Those late and last-second additions doomed the U.S. Men's National Team that went to the 1998 World Cup. Tony DiCicco, coach of the U.S. Women's National Team at the time, noted that the older players welcomed the younger players of the women's team as a way of improving the overall ability of the team. Concerning the men's team of 1998, he said that the older guys "had no connection to those on the field." John Harkes shows how correct DiCicco was in Harkes' autobiography *Captain for Life*. He wrote several times that qualifying for the 1998 World Cup involved bringing in some younger players, resulting in him and other veterans playing less. Harkes tells of a meeting after a national team game in 1997. After those newer players left the locker room, the older players talked to Steve Sampson about his lineup changes. Harkes explained that players were added to the team after the U.S. had qualified for the World Cup. Those new guys, wrote Harkes, "had a trip to (the World Cup) handed to them on a silver platter."

How old was Eddie Gaven when he first played for the U.S. Men's National team?
Appearing in a national team game—known as earning a cap—usually follows a couple weeks of veterans and rookies training together. In November 2004, during qualifying for the 2006 World Cup, that mix had veterans Kasey Keller and Jonny Walker running around with the

team's youngest player, Eddie Gaven. Videographer Mark
Thomas explained that the three often ate dinner together
"at restaurants where a 17-year-old has no clue what to
order." At those restaurants Gaven often got surprised. The
veterans repeatedly were telling the restaurant staffs that
Gaven was celebrating his birthday, bringing out waiters
and waitresses singing to Gaven.

**Thomas Dooley earned 81 caps with the United States.
How old was he when he first played for the United
States?**
Dooley could be the asterisk to the question about the first
American to play in the Bundesliga. He was born and
raised in Germany, playing in the country's top division in
1986, before becoming a U.S. citizen. His American father
enabled him to gain citizenship in 1992 and vie for a spot
with the U.S. National Team. He made his first appearance
with the national team in May 1992, just after turning 31
years old. The following year he was named the U.S.
Player of the Year.

**Of the men who have played for the U.S. Men's
National Team, which has the most appearances?**
When the North American Soccer League folded, he
figured that his soccer career would be over after high
school, where he lettered in two other sports. Nevertheless
Cobi Jones made the soccer team at UCLA as a walk-on
and later played a little in Europe and South America and
then on the 1992 U.S. Olympic Team. His first match for
the U.S. Men's National Team was in September 1992. At
the end of 2005, he had 164 appearances, which also puts
him third among all international players on Earth.

**What man has the most caps for the United States
without ever appearing in a World Cup game?**
As of the end of 2005, seven people had played for the U.S.

10 or more times without once playing in a World Cup. Chris Armas leads them all with 66 caps. Jovan Kirovski has 62; Rick Davis, 36; Angelo DiBernardo, 20; Arnie Mausser, 35; Willy Roy, 19; and Ed Murphy, 17. The winner, or loser, of this category, was almost Hugo Perez. He was a mainstay for the U.S. Men's National Team during the lean years and was left home when Coach Bob Gansler picked his roster for the 1990 World Cup. However, Perez returned to the national team after 1990, reached 72 caps, and was named to the roster that played in the 1994 World Cup. He spent the first three matches of the World Cup on the bench, though, stuck at 72 caps without one minute of World Cup playing time. Finally, he got into his one and only World Cup match to face Brazil. The U.S. lost that game, getting knocked out of the tournament, and Perez appeared for the national team never again.

Who was the first American man to earn 100 caps?
He also was the 1992 and 1994 U.S. Soccer Male Athlete of the Year. He's Marcela Balboa.

Who was the first woman to appear for the U.S. Women's National Team in 100 games?
Mia Hamm refers to this woman as her hero. Hamm's hero started her national team career for the United States two weeks after turning 16 years old in August 1987. Kristine Lilly kept playing through her 100th national team appearance, which came in 1996, She earned her 200th cap in 2000 and is still playing today.

At what position did Nicole Barnhart earn her first cap for the U.S. Women's National Team?
When the U.S. Women's National Team ran out of subs in a match that was part of the 2004 Fan Celebration Tour, Barnhart, a goalkeeper, played the final four minutes as a

forward. She later earned her first cap in goal at the 2005
Algarve Cup, recording a shut-out.

**What stat did Tiffany Roberts gain in the first five
minutes of her first U.S. Women's National Team
appearance?**
Within minutes of her start against Portugal, in March
1994, Roberts earned a caution. As a 16-year-old, though,
she had a long career ahead of her. She went on to appear
109 more times for the U.S.

**Who's this? She graduated from high school in three
years. She has scored more goals in the history of
University of North Carolina women's soccer than
anybody else. In her national team debut, she scored
two goals against Russia.**
She also scored back-to-back hat tricks in June 2000, the
year she led the women's national team with 19 goals.
Cindy Parlow also scored four goals against England in a
2003 game. Even though she missed some national team
games due to school responsibilities for a couple years,
Parlow became just the fifth player in U.S. history to record
60 international goals.

**How many women played for the U.S. in all four of the
first four Women's World Cups?**
The first four women's World Cups were played in 1991,
1995, 1999, and 2003. Mia Hamm, Julie Foudy, Kristine
Lilly, and Joy Biefeld Fawcett played in all of them. Of
those women, two stand a chance of playing in the 2007
Women's World Cup, Lilly and Fawcett. Lilly has
remained active with the team and has played in over 300
games for the U.S. Fawcett—the only player to play every
minute of the World Cups of 1995, 1999, and 2003—left
the team after 2003 but returned in 2005.

Who are the only men to be named to four World Cup rosters for the U.S.?

Considering that the United States' first four World Cup appearances were spread from 1930 to 1990, it's a safe bet that these two men did it recently. Prior to 2006, a handful of men had played in three World Cups. Earnie Stewart, Claudio Reyna, and Cobi Jones played in the World Cups of 1994, 1998, and 2002. Tony Meola was on the rosters of 1990, 1994, and 2002, while Kasey Keller made the team in 1990, 1998, and 2002. When the roster was finalized for 2006, it included Reyna and Keller, making them the only men to make U.S. teams for four men's World Cups.

Through 2006 what goalkeeper has played the most games in the World Cup for the United States Men's National Team?

Brad Friedel played in all five of the U.S.'s games during the 2002 World Cup in Asia. However, those are the only ones he has played in. Kasey Keller played in the three games of the 1998 World Cup and the three games in 2006. The difference is that Tony Meola played in the four games of the 1994 World Cup and the three games of the 1990 finals, giving him a total of seven.

Among all players throughout the history of FIFA, who has played in the most international games?

Her biography is staggering. She's Cal Ripken with trophies. The highlights of women's soccer include her earning all-tournament team and MVP honors. She scored big goals for the United States and headed one away. She became the most capped player ever, man or woman, on May 21, 1998, when she played in her 152nd international game. She reached her 200th national team appearance two years later. She has remained healthy for the most part as she has beaten younger women and their replacements for starting spots on the team. As 2006 began, she had played in 85 percent of all U.S. Women's National Team games ever. If Kristine Lilly had actually stopped playing, other international players would know where the bar was set. She and Mia Hamm started their national team careers at the same time, but when Hamm retired in 2004, Lilly kept going. As of January 2007, Lilly had 319 caps and was still playing for the United States.

Media

Who was the first soccer player from a professional league in the United States to appear on The Tonight Show?
Two years prior to joining the NASL, Pele appeared on The Tonight Show. His second appearance in 1975—after joining the NASL—was more notable. Having trouble with English but still understanding most of the conversation, Pele's second visit was with Bert Convey, the guest host. After Convey asked if the United States would ever see the violent side of soccer that the rest of the world experiences, Pele answered, "Yes, I think so."

Media coverage of what 1990s event was called shameful and irresponsible by *Detroit Free Press* sports columnist Mitch Albom?
Albom, often voted the best sports columnist by sports editors across the country, considered media coverage of the 1999 Women's World Cup to be too much jumping on the bandwagon. He expressed no qualms with sports writers who follow the pack in demeaning soccer.

Who was the first professional soccer player to get on the cover of *Sports Illustrated*?
Two years before Pele came into the NASL, Bob Rigby, goalkeeper of the Philadelphia Atoms, appeared on the

cover on September 3, 1973. Philadelphia was tearing up the league that year, on its way to winning the league title behind Rigby and several other American players. The photo caption is "Soccer Goes American". In the background of the photo are the stripes from a football field interrupting the soccer field. It was the first cover story on soccer for the magazine that started in 1954. Long before the magazine put soccer on the cover, it had chess (1961), lacrosse (1962), and archery (1963).

Who was the first American-born scoring champion of the NASL and the person labeled by *Sports Illustrated* in August 1973 as the "Great American Hope" for soccer? Perhaps the most overlooked story in American soccer is the one of Kyle Rote Jr. He excelled in football, baseball, and basketball as a youngster and started playing soccer when he was 16 to keep in shape. His football skills earned him high school All-American status and a scholarship to Oklahoma State University, where he enrolled in 1968. His plans were to follow his father through college and into the National Football League. Months into his college experience, Rote became disheartened with the training camp atmosphere of O.S.U. and was framed by teammates for stealing. He left O.S.U., transferring to the University of the South at Sewanee. He succeeded within the young Sewanee soccer program and got noticed by NASL scouts. The Dallas Tornado drafted him as its first pick in 1972 with the intention of working with a local player with potential. In 1973 he led the league in goal scoring and was named rookie of the year. He stayed with Dallas through 1978, then headed to the Houston Hurricane. He played for the U.S. National Team several times as well.

What common image was on the cover of *Time*, *Newsweek*, *People*, and *Sports Illustrated* in mid-July 1999?

During June and July 1999, the United States of America was a household of patriotic soccer lovers, and the favorite daughters were the ones on the U.S. team. The drama mounted through the final game, pitting the Americans-next-door against China on a Saturday afternoon six days after July 4. Dragging the suspense to a maximum level, the darlings of sport showed the world that the U.S. was the greatest nation on earth in terms of women's soccer if not everything else. The story brought cover shots on all four of those magazines, and *Sports Illustrated* later named the team athletes of the year.

Goalkeeper Shep Messing made some money by posing nude for a magazine while he was playing in the NASL. Which magazine?

Messing was a literal poster boy. During his senior year at Harvard, he did some modeling work in Boston. As a professional goalkeeper, he appeared naked in *Viva* magazine. Messing said that the league's press releases generated less publicity for soccer than "dropping my pants."

How many people died due to violence that occurred during the 1994 World Cup?

When England got put out during the qualifying stages, tournament organizers raised a few glasses. Conventional wisdom held that without England, violence would be less likely during the World Cup. Media fools who had criticized the tournament for the violence it would bring were forced to disrespect soccer in other ways. They picked on the low scores and the odd names—real mature stuff. They did not report on any deaths due to violence during the tournament: none happened. Two people associated with the tournament did lose their lives. One was a police officer training for potential terrorist attacks before the tournament. The other was Andres Escobar, a Columbian player.

Who was Brian Budd and how did he kill ABC Sports' "Superstars" competition?

Within the soccer world, Budd was a national team player for Canada. In a qualifying game for the 1978 World Cup, he scored the first goal against the U.S. and led Canada in a 3-0 victory that ended the U.S. effort to reach the World Cup. Within the minds of people who paid little attention to soccer, Budd was trouble for a different reason. After seeing domestic interest in pitting athletes from a range of sports against each other, ABC added a "Superstars" competition for women, teams, Canada, Great Britain, and others distinctions. Budd, also an NASL player, won the Canadian version of "Superstars", qualifying for the world "Superstars". He won the larger competition in 1978, 1979, and 1980, ceremonially earning the title of best athlete in the world. Within the hyperbole of the made-by-TV event, it sparked debate and generated some attention about the claim that soccer players were the best athletes. What it also did was turn Americans off "Superstars" since their heroes were not doing too well. So ABC decided to retire Budd, causing another rift about its treatment of Canadian athletes. The competitions ended quietly soon after.

Which English-language U.S. cable channel regularly showed games from the Major Indoor Soccer League in the early 1980s?

It was not ESPN or any other all-sports network. It was the USA Network.

Which English-language U.S. cable channel showed the most games of the 1990 World Cup?

It was not ESPN or any other all-sports network. It was

TNT, which showed 24 matches. Even though the cable station reached only a portion of the U.S., each game was watched by an average of 571,000 homes. That step into sports broadcasting continued with TNT bidding on NFL games a couple years later, encouraging the NFL to start a weekly Sunday night game. It became a huge revenue generator for the league and television broadcasters.

Which network in the 1980s regular televised soccer games from Germany?

Keep in mind that this was a time that most households received three networks and the public station. Even when ESPN and the first cable channels came along, you were lucky to find one game per week. And without a VCR, which few people owned, you had to set your schedule to the television if you wanted to catch a game. With education as its objective, the Public Broadcasting Service took a game each week from the German leagues, cut it down to 60 minutes, and showed it commercial-free. Saturday Night Live once poked fun at this, spoofing a PBS pledge drive by threatening more soccer if people refused to give more money.

Who's this? He played soccer at Harvard and became the program's assistant coach. He started providing play-by-play for soccer games on a Boston television station and then called games on the radio for the Boston Minutemen and the New York Cosmos of the NASL. He went on to work games for the broadcasters of World Cups and big games on ABC, CBS, NBC, ESPN, and ESPN2.

His is likely the most familiar voice among soccer fans in the U.S. The accent gives him away. He's Seamus Malin, winner of the 2005 Colin Jose Media Award of the National Soccer Hall of Fame. The only previous winner, Jerry Trecker, is known for his contributions as a mainstream columnist covering soccer for the West Hartford News from 1955 through 1975 and then contributing to ESPN, ABC, and PBS.

What do these events have to do with Major League Soccer: the death of Pope John Paul II, the death of Ronald Reagan, and the death of John F. Kennedy Jr.?
Major League Soccer seems to have caught the O.J. jinx from the 1994 World Cup. With top network coverage still rare for MLS soccer games, the three deaths managed to knock the wind out of MLS executives by commandeering the network air. JFK Jr.'s death in 1999 replaced ABC's live telecast of the MLS all-star game. In 2004, ABC bumped a Chicago/D.C. game to ESPN to cover Reagan's death. Then the Pope's passing in 2005 pushed the league's 10th opening game from ABC to ESPN. The coincidence goes one step further. On Oct. 7, 2001, ABC was planning live coverage of the U.S. Men's National Team's World Cup qualifier against Jamaica. The U.S. won the game 2-1, earning a ticket to the finals in Asia. However, the game was shown later on ESPN, because ABC was broadcasting coverage of the U.S. military invasion of Afghanistan.

How did TNT handle the need for commercials during play of the 1990 World Cup?
For a long time continuous play was a reason cited by anti-soccer people that soccer would not succeed in the U.S. Broadcasters could not fit in enough commercials. The F&M Schaefer Brewing Company showed commercials during the International Soccer League games in 1960. *The New York Times* explained that the broadcasters superimposed "modest commercials over the action on the field." In 1967 CBS televised some NPSL games by using goal kicks and injuries to run commercials. That led to some situations where referees discouraged quick recoveries and encouraged long delays on restarts. For the

1990 World Cup, TNT shrunk the view of the games into a smaller area, adding a commercial border around the action. Budweiser's logo was shown in that border, and the commentators noted the sponsor for providing the game commercial-free.

What percentage of U.S. residents watched some of the 1994 World Cup on television?
Played within the U.S., the 1994 World Cup received more attention from U.S. television audiences than any previous World Cup. According to a Harris Poll, 44 percent watched at least some of the tournament.

How many million people in the United States watched the final game of the Women's World Cup in 1999?
Packed into the Rose Bowl were 90,185 people, a world record for women's sporting events. Watching on television in the U.S. were 40 million.

Three days after the U.S. won the 1999 Women's World Cup, the U.S. men played a match in Denver. There a woman impersonated one of the women's team players and nearly got away with it. Who was she impersonating?
Trying to get away with posing as Mia Hamm or Michelle Akers or Brandi Chastain would have been too risky. The woman walked in front of the crowd pretending to be Kristine Lilly, the most capped player in the history of the world but also one of the least recognized. When Bryan Chenault, part of the United States Soccer Federation staff, confronted the woman, she stuck to her story. He then told a security guard that the woman was an imposter. The guard replied, "Who cares? The crowd loves her."

Fans

True or False? During Pele's last season with the New York Cosmos, the team's game attendance was below what it had been prior to his arrival.
In 1974, the year before he joined the team, the Cosmos' home attendance averaged 3,500 per game. That rose to over 10,000 in 1975, boosted by Pele's arrival in June. In 1976 the average went to over 18,000. It kept climbing in 1977, his final year with the Cosmos, to above 34,000. The away attendance for Cosmos games was similar—from 7,100 to almost 14,000 to above 21,000 to over 25,000. The leagues attendance was lifted overall during the Pele years. In 1977 it was about 13,500 people per game, compared to 1974's 7,500. In 1974 attendance was so poor that the Washington Diplomats fired their public relations director, threatened to revoke press credentials to a *Washington Post* reporter, and refused to sell *Soccer Weekly*, because they would not perpetuate the exaggeration that one specific night's attendance was higher than the naked eye would support. The exaggeration was that 3,325 people were at the game.

In thousands what was the average attendance at New York Cosmos' games in 1978?
The team's attendance for its early years was appalling. In 1974 it was 3,500. Of course, that was before Pele, who played there in 1975, 1976, and 1977. During his final season, attendance topped ten times what it had been in 1974. In 1978, though, it got even better. The team averaged almost 48,000.

Which was the best attended World Cup in history?
In terms of attendance, the 1994 World Cup had nearly 3.6 million people attending the 52 games, an average of almost 69,000 people per game. Four years earlier in Italy,

the 52 games brought in 2.5 million people. Four years
before that, the 1986 World Cup in Mexico had 2.4 million
people in the stands of its 52 games. Starting in 1998, FIFA
added eight teams, creating 12 more games. Nevertheless,
the 1998 World Cup in France had only 2.8 million people;
Asia's 2002 World Cup had 2.7 million; and Germany
brought in 3.35 million.

**What is the name of the unofficial fan club for the
United States Men's National Team?**
Following the 1994 World Cup, Mark Spacone and John
Wright decided that the U.S. Men's National Team needed
some leadership for crowd support. Inviting other fans, the
two led cheers, chants, and songs for the first time in
Foxboro, Massachusetts, when the U.S. met Nigeria in June
1995. They developed a name to honor Uncle Sam—Sam's
Army—and developed a modus operandi: wear red, stand
throughout the game, buy seats behind one of the end lines.
The group maintains a web site, www.sams-army.com with
information on joining and plans for the future.

What team led the MLS in away attendance in 2004?
With the addition of the Freddy Adu, the youngest player to
ever play in the league, D.C. United became a hot ticket
when the team went on the road. The team averaged
23,686 per game, the highest in the league by more than
6,000 people. That interest in Adu created a jump in league
attendance overall, bringing in 4% more people in 2004
than the league had in 2003.

**Which New York venue hosted Pele's first game with
the Cosmos?**
The team started out in Yankee Stadium in 1971, the first
year in operation. A year later the team played at Hofstra
University on Long Island. In 1974 they moved again, this
time to Downing Stadium on Randall's Island, where Pele

played his first game for the team. Then they went back to Yankee Stadium in 1976 to accommodate the larger crowds. A year later the Cosmos moved to Giants Stadium in New Jersey.

What event led FIFA to allow the organizers of the 1999 Women's World Cup to hold the games in the United States' largest stadiums instead of smaller college stadiums?
Prior to the 1996 Olympic Games, FIFA was set on having the Women's World Cup games played in smaller stadiums. The world governing body anticipated sparse crowds and exorbitant costs with the U.S.'s largest venues. Having seen the organizing and marketing power of the U.S. during the 1994 World Cup but more importantly having experienced the crowds for women's games during the 1996 Olympic Games, FIFA gave in to U.S. organizers and allowed them to book the largest venues in the States.

What was historically different about the stadium that the United States and Switzerland played in during the 1994 World Cup?
The Pontiac Silverdome, by being a venue of the 1994 tournament, became the first indoor venue of a World Cup game. To comply with the need to play on grass, Silverdome staff grew natural turf outside and pieced it together on platforms inside.

Which MLS team was the first to build its own stadium?
In 1967 the National Professional Soccer League lost $600,000. After the league merged with the United Soccer Association to create the NASL, teams still bled cash, paying big money to accommodate 20,000 people in 60,000-seat stadiums. The problem persisted through other professional leagues and into the days of Major League

Soccer. The solution was daunting—build venues specifically for soccer and quit paying rent for unnecessary seating—because of the cost. Working with government entities, the Columbus Crew built its own stadium and opened it in 1999. The Los Angeles Galaxy followed, opening The Home Depot Center in 2003. Then Dallas finished Pizza Hut Park in 2005. The bottom-line immediately improved for each of those teams, leading the Galaxy to announce a $150,000 profit after its first year in its new home.

In what stadium did Tim Howard make his first start for Manchester United?
During the summer of 2003, Howard signed a deal to leave the New York/New Jersey MetroStars to play for Manchester United. The contract was finalized just as ManU was embarking on a U.S. tour. That enabled Howard to play his first game for his new team in Giants Stadium, just miles from where he had grown up.

Business

Why didn't soccer pick back up after the Great Depression?
The best explanation comes from the book *Offside: Soccer & American Exceptionalism*. The authors feel that since soccer had not caught on during the blossoming of the United States—late 1800s and early 1900s—it was doomed. The "sport space" became filled with baseball, football, and basketball. The next real attempt to bring the game to the U.S. came during the Cold War, when every American was expected to be suspicious of anything from a foreign country. Clive Toye explained it pretty well. He was the president of the New York Cosmos. Once asked by a reporter why the Cosmos gave out so many incentives to

draw attendance, Toye explained popular perception in the U.S.: People believed that any athlete who kicked a ball instead of caught one was "a Commie or a fairy."

What executive is credited with turning around the NASL?

Coming from England to run the league's Atlanta team, Phil Woosnam became commissioner of the NASL between the 1970 and 1971 seasons. He realized the importance of having a team in New York because of the influence of the New York media. He succeeded by getting Warner Communications to start a team called the Cosmos. From there attention picked up and more teams joined the league.

What brand of shoe did Pele wear while playing for the Cosmos?

This is almost humorous to think that the greatest player to play soccer in the U. S. wore a brand on his feet that nobody under 30 remembers. Nevertheless, in 1976 when Pele scored the 1250th goal of his career, he was handed a gold shoe complete with the Pony logo.

What company owned the New England Tea Men of the NASL?

The name makes sense for two reasons: there's the tea revolt of centuries gone by and the fact that Lipton Tea actually owned the team. The name made less sense when the team moved from Boston to Jacksonville, Florida, for the 1981 season.

How many MLS teams had no owners when the league began in 1996?

When Major League Soccer opened in 1996 with ten teams, the structure for ownership was that each team would be 51 percent held by the league and 49 percent held by an owner-operator. Seven of the original 10 teams had owner-operators working in partnership with the league. Three teams were entirely owned by the league and operated by the league. They were Tampa Bay, Dallas, and San Jose.

What is the difference between the NASL and MLS that has kept MLS teams from bidding wars for the top players?

NASL teams became victims of their own arms race. "It became fashionable to chase the Cosmos," said San Diego Sockers President Jack Daley in a 1984 *Sports Illustrated* article. "Everyone had to have a Pele," Daley said. Coaches searched for comparable players and paid them to come to the U.S., consequently raising the payroll of NASL teams. In 1979 the Cosmos had a payroll of $9.4 million. In their effort to compete, NASL teams overspent, encouraging other teams to overspend. Revenues could not support that overspending, leading teams to fold or continue to overspend, assuming that more expensive players would yield higher attendance. Just prior to the 1984 season, owners and players agreed to a graduated salary cap, but it was too late. To prevent a repeat of that display of human nature, Major League Soccer was set up as a single entity—one company. Teams do not pay players; the league does. That eliminates the competition to pull players into the league and the competition among MLS teams to offer higher salaries. Major League Soccer assigns each player to a team and posts that player's wages against the team's total player salary. Every team has the same maximum limit that its teams can "spend" on players' salaries. The only exception is the Beckham rule, which is far too complex to explain here.

How much money did Alan Rothenberg receive as a bonus for running the 1994 World Cup?

Soccer players in the U.S. may not have the salaries of those in baseball, football, and basketball. In 2005, Landon

Donovan was the supposed top MLS earner at $900,000.
However, for being the CEO of the 1994 World Cup, Alan
Rothenberg was given a big-league salary—$7 million.
When he had taken the reigns of running the show, the
whole world thought that the tournament would flop inside
empty stadiums. Instead, the 52 games were witnessed by
3.5 million people, and they generated a $60 million profit.
Nevertheless his going-away present generated a lot of
criticism because Rothenberg was the president of the
United States Soccer Federation at the time and used
thousands of volunteers to staff the tournament.

**What happened to the largest chunk of the profit from
the 1994 World Cup?**
Most of it became the endowment for the United States
Soccer Foundation, a non-profit organization created to
"enhance, assist, and grow" soccer in the U.S. The
foundation provides grants and loans that have sustained
leagues, built fields, and provided equipment.

**What American-based business, known best for its
drink, helped get the Cosmos in the door to talk to Pele
about playing soccer in the United States?**
With global appeal, Pele drew attention from global
companies. In 1971 that global appeal brought Pepsi execs
to sign Pele to lead the Pepsi Kids campaign. As he
traveled with Santos on tours throughout the world, Pele
conducted soccer clinics with the backing of Pepsi.
Through Pepsi, Cosmos executives contacted Pele about
playing in the United States. When he got here, part of his
contract with Warner Communications, the owner of the
Cosmos, was that Pele would add to his product concerns.
During the first year with the team, Pele pitched for
miniature soccer games, shoes, balls, shin guards, lunch
kits, and novelty hats. He went on to appear with Jimmy
Connors and Muhammad Ali to sell cologne, and he pushed

Honda's off-road bikes and motorcycles. Also he did two
classics: a Lite beer commercial as part of the great taste/
less filling series and an American Express commercial—
one of those that asked *Do you know me*?

**With the beginning of the Municipal Amateur Soccer
League of St. Louis in 1912, two men promised to
provide trophies to the winners of the 18-team league.
One of them was William T. Collins, manager of the
local office of the A.G. Spalding Sporting Goods
Company. Who was the other person?**
Soccer players and fans should not be surprised to hear how
beer was such a part of soccer in St. Louis. Adolphus A.
Busch, president of Anheuser-Busch Brewery, was the other
person who promised to provide a trophy.

**What brand was the first official sponsor of Major
League Soccer?**
St. Louis had a long beer history and a long soccer history.
The Municipal Amateur Soccer League operated for 44
years and the Catholic Youth Council has run its own
league for kids and adults since 1956. The city had its own
professional soccer leagues from 1891 through 1938 and
again from1947 through 1953. During much of that time,
teams and leagues enjoyed the support of beer companies
such as Anheuser Busch, Fallstaff, Griesedieck, and
Carling. Anheuser-Busch was the big dog, though. It
partnered with the St. Louis Stars of the NASL and
sponsored the World Cups of 1986, 1990, and 1994. When
MLS went looking for corporate partners, Anheuser-Busch
paid for Budweiser to be the league's official beer.

**For years goalkeeper Shep Messing endorsed what
tobacco product?**
Messing never hid his extroverted personality. He had the
body and character for marketing and earned several

endorsement deals. The oddest was his commitment to push Skoal chewing tobacco. By contrast, Rick Davis, the boy next door, made commercials that had him showering with Ivory soap.

Fouls

What U.S. college is credited with placing soccer behind football in U.S. popularity?

Within a couple years of the first soccer match ever played between U.S. colleges, Rutgers, Princeton, Columbia, Yale, and Stevens created an informal league that forbade picking up, throwing, and carrying the ball. Representatives of those teams met in 1873 to further formalize their rules. What resulted was a guide for a kicking game quite similar to the game being codified by England's Football Association. Harvard refused to attend the meeting, though, favoring their Boston Game, which was popular among Harvard students and people who lived nearby. It allowed the use of hands, tackling opponents, and taxing everything. As the lone hold-out with its Boston game, Harvard held matches among its students until May 1874, when it hosted Canada's McGill University. They played two games in Cambridge, the first under the rules of the Boston game and the second under McGill's modified rugby rules. Harvard won the first, tied the second, and created a wave of support for proving American superiority. Before 1880 the five other schools converted their teams in order to challenge Harvard for that superiority.

Which president can we blame for soccer's second-class status?

Soccer had a shot at being placed above American football in the first years of the 20th Century. It was being played in some colleges, but as a fall/winter sport it was second in popularity to American football. The fall of 1904 brought media to explore the darker side of American football: win-at-all-cost coaches, ineligible players, revenue-driven scheduling, team-jumping players, injuries, and violence. Some colleges were closing their American football programs and banning the game among its own students. President Theodore Roosevelt had played American football in college, considering it a character builder and a healthy activity. He said that he saw the game as a means of keeping a person prepared to defend himself and the nation. Concerned about increasing injuries, the number of schools switching to rugby and soccer, and the media uprising against American football, Roosevelt invited football representatives from Harvard, Yale, and Princeton to the White House in October 1905. (During the 1905 season, 18 college players and 46 high school students would die playing American football, reported the *Chicago Tribune*.) Roosevelt told the coaches to fix the game. Those coaches then met with several New York Area college representatives in December to decide if the game should be repaired or replaced. By a narrow margin, they followed Roosevelt's call and chose to repair it. They then scheduled another meeting to return with more college representatives from the East and Mid-west. That second meeting led to a rules reform committee that proposed changes and created the Intercollegiate Athletic Association. It was renamed the National Collegiate Athletic Association in 1910.

Has Harvard ever won an NCAA men's college championship in soccer?
After snubbing the sport in the latest years of the 19th Century, Harvard restarted a men's soccer program in 1905 and continued it through 1916 to be picked up for good in 1928. But keep mind that these were the guys who whacked the legs out from under the game: they did not

deserve to win a national title in soccer. The closest the
Crimson ever got was in 1969 and 1971, when the team
reached the NCAA semifinals.

Can we blame FIFA for the fact that American football is more popular than soccer is in the U.S.?

Traditionally FIFA has been concerned about adult soccer
and the leagues that govern adult soccer. The OPEC of the
game had no time for college games or, for that matter,
youth games. Also, keep in mind that FIFA is un-
American. People ridicule and despise the NCAA's heavy
handedness even though it's run by U.S. college
administrators and is headquartered in Indianapolis. Just
think how the average college president felt when he was
being given orders from Europe-based FIFA during the days
that followed World War I and during the time that the U.S.
Congress was snubbing its nose at joining the League of
Nations. We can run our own sports leagues, thank you. If
we have to deal with you for soccer, we'll get back to you
in a few decades.

Can we blame colleges?

For years colleges were the biggest investors in soccer in
the United States and were the feeder program for the U.S.
Men's National Team. By contrast the rest of the world
was developing soccer players through clubs. The first
problem with college soccer is that the additional criteria—
enrollment qualifications, grades, fraternity parties—
prohibit some good players from being eligible for teams.
In other nations there is one criterion to play organized
soccer—ability. There also is the fact that college coaches
are expected to win, not develop quality soccer players.
That drive to win without concern for what the player
becomes has led coaches to encourage physical play,
employ defensive tactics, and recruit foreigners who take
spots away from U.S. citizens. Another disadvantage,

wrote Claudio Reyna, "is that players are competing mainly with their peers." The U.S.'s 1990 World Cup team found itself playing against 15-year professional veterans who were eating 18-year-olds for lunch every weekend and regularly scoring goals on the most legendary goalkeepers. Reyna also noted problems with the NCAA's ban on players playing for club teams while college is in session. That means that even though the college soccer season ends in December, players cannot work out with club teams until May. Bruce Arena, a former college coach, weighed in about college programs, in *Soccer America* in 2004: "We need to have our youth development for our top players" provided by professional clubs, not colleges.

Can we blame the United States Soccer Federation?
Certainly we can blame the USSF some. Come on, you can't hold all the authority of soccer without being blamed correctly for what goes wrong. Of course, the USSF was hindered by its membership in FIFA, keeping it from adapting the game for colleges, where American football and basketball grew. However, nothing hindered the USSF from developing players younger than college age. Focused so much on adult tournaments, the USSF paid passing attention to developing future players until the late 1960s when kids started mimicking what they were seeing in the NASL. An effort in 1971 to address youth soccer fell flat when the USSF sought to tax every registered player $1 with the money going toward a youth soccer development program. First off, this was 1971. National attention to youth soccer should have been decades old by then. Second, many of the adults liked the idea but didn't want to pay for it. "We understand money is needed for this program," wrote the executive secretary of the Old Tymers Soccer Association of St. Louis. He then stated that other funding mechanisms should be found. Within its efforts to serve all ages, the USSF suffered from administrative

problems as well. Joel Cohen wrote a paper in 1993 as part of his studies at Boston University exploring the marketing history of soccer in the United States. He quotes a few professional business people who were involved in soccer. They considered the USSF for many years to be amateurish, political, parochial, and incompetent. One business person blamed the organization for "stunting the growth of soccer in the 1980s." Cohen goes on to express that many people in leadership positions treated those positions as rewards for service instead of expectations of action.

What about the average person? Can we blame them too?

Sure. We expect youth sports in the United States to be governed by schools. The Amateur Athletic Union was the exception but has taken a back seat to state secondary school athletic associations, the NCAA, and NAIA. Nowhere else in the world do athletics and education bind themselves together as tightly. After education became compulsory, Americans grew to expect lunch, condoms, and many other needs to be handled by schools.

Can we blame the media?

Jack Flamhaft did. He was president of the American Soccer League and was quoted in *Sports Illustrated*'s November 28, 1955, edition as saying, "Games are grudgingly covered." In the same issue, Roy Stambaugh, captain of Ohio State University's soccer team, said, "[Soccer's] growth is seriously hindered by the lack of publicity." Terry Springthorpe, captain of the New York Americans, said, "There is no backing from the press." To be fair, in 1955 soccer was such a blip on the sports screen that it didn't deserve much more coverage than it got. However, the coverage did not keep up as the game became more popular. Then there is the media attitude that encourages ridiculing the game. That is inexcusable. Other than sports writer, what other area of journalism allows its professionals to demean the subject they cover?

Out of Our Hands: Luck, Superstition, and Coincidence

Brandi Chastain missed a penalty kick against China months prior to the 1999 Women's World Cup. As she took a penalty kick in the final of the World Cup, what two things did she do differently compared to the earlier PK?
First, she avoided eye contact with the Chinese 'keeper the second time. Second she switched feet. The March 1999 penalty kick was missed with her right foot. When Chastain was told by Assistant Coach Lauren Gregg that she would be taking a penalty kick during the shootout of the World Cup final, Gregg told her to take it left footed. She did and scored.

The U.S. Women's National Team throughout much of the 1990s would do a cheer just before games. It was *yousah, yousah, yousah*. What does that mean?
If the initials of their country were put together as if they spelled a word, that word phonetically would be something like *yousah* but spelled U.S.A.

What was Mia Hamm's pre-game meal?
Hamm admits to being quiet and intense prior to games. She does not have a standard ritual "other than eating my usual pre-game, peanut-butter-and-jelly sandwich."

During the penalty kick tie-breaker of the 1999 Women's World Cup final, what did goalkeeper Brianna Scurry do to the third kicker before the kick?
Brianna Scurry remembers that prior to the start of the

shootout, she had confidence in her teammates to successfully score their five shots. To come out ahead, Scurry felt that she had to save just one of the shots from her opponents. She failed to save the first shot and then the second. Not since she had been 15 years old had she looked at a shooter before a PK. She tried it to the third Chinese kicker, Liu Ying, and it worked. Scurry saved the kick by diving left, giving the U.S. a 3-2 lead after each team had taken three shots.

What U.S. player scored on her own team in the 1999 Women's World Cup?

With a full stadium of voices in the team's quarterfinal match against Germany, Brandi Chastain and goalie Brianna Scurry had a tough time communicating. Chastain pushed the ball back to where Scurry had just been and had to watch it roll into the net. The game had the potential to be a nail-biting, one-goal contest, but the U.S. managed to come back once to tie the game and then to tie it again at 2-2. That second goal was scored by Chastain. The U.S. ended up adding another goal to win 3-2.

What prevented the United States from giving up a goal in golden-goal overtime to China in the final match of the 1999 Women's World Cup?

Kristine Lilly has often guarded a post on opponents' corner kicks. She did that day and watched a ball beat goalkeeper Brianna Scurry and head her direction. Scurry remembers watching the ball get past her as she thought "oh shit". A goal would give China the World Cup championship. Lilly headed the ball back to be cleared by Brandi Chastain. The game continued and eventually went down to penalty kicks.

Why did the United States become the host of the 2003 Women's World Cup after China had been selected previously?

With the games scheduled to be played in China in September and October 2003, FIFA's Executive Committee decided to move the finals out of China because of its difficulty containing Severe Acute Respiratory Syndrome, SARS. Three weeks after making the announcement, the executive committee chose the U.S. as host, giving organizers four months to plan the tournament.

Where was Slodubian Djordjevic when he was asked to play for the United States Men's National Team in a 1974 World Cup qualifier?
On September 10, 1972, the U.S. took on Mexico in Los Angeles. Mexico had qualified for the next round and the U.S. was knocked out. According to Roger Allaway and Colin Jose, who wrote *The United States Tackles the World Cup*, Djordjevic was in the stadium to watch the match when he was recognized by some of the U.S. players as a member of a strong New York club. They asked him to play in the game, and he ended up starting in what was his only appearance for the U.S.

Did Japan play in the 1994 World Cup?
With a 2-1 lead in the last match of qualifying, Japan seemed to be headed to the U.S. for the 1994 World Cup. It would have been the nation's first ever trip to the tournament. Japan gave up a goal to Iraq, however, with seconds left in the game. The tie game put Japan in a tie for the second, and final, of Asia's qualifying spots. However, on goal differential, South Korea beat out Japan and headed to the U.S. Four years later, Japan was drawn into the same group as South Korea, only one of which would get a direct berth into the 1998 finals. South Korea won the group, leaving Japan to play Iran for the last Asian spot. Leading 1-0 at half, Japan let the game be tied and reached full time with a 2-2 deadlock. An extra time goal sent Japan to France for its first ever trip to the World Cup.

Prior to the 1999 Women's World Cup semifinal between the United States and Brazil, why did Mia Hamm get upset with teammate Tisha Venturini?
Venturini sat in the wrong spot in the locker room. Hamm had established a superstition during the tournament of sitting between Kristine Lilly and Carla Overbeck only to find Venturini altering that arrangement. Hamm gave Venturini a look that everybody on the team knew, and Venturini relinquished the seat.

In the U.S. game against Portugal during the 2002 World Cup, the same explanation is given for two of the five goals. What is it?
Looking to add a goal to the U.S.'s 1-0 lead, Landon Donovan tackled a ball away from a Portugal defender and sent a cross into the penalty area. Soon after it left Donovan's foot, the ball deflected off Portugal's Jorge Costa and dropped between the goalie and the cross bar. It was credited as an own goal. In the 71st minute, with the game 3-1, U.S. defender Jeff Agoos knocked a ball into his own goal, making the second own goal in one game. After the game, Agoos told the media about an e-mail he had received from a friend before the game. His friend had predicted that Agoos would score. Agoos told reporters, "I'm going to tell him to be more specific for the next one."

Why was South Korea's Park Ji Sung a hero to the United States during the 2002 World Cup?
While the Yanks were trailing Poland in the final game of group play, South Korea and Portugal were scoreless. The situation suited South Korea and Portugal since both would be granted passage to the next round. By contrast that coupling of results would have knocked out the U.S. Everything changed after two Portugal players were ejected. Park scored, sending up eruptions of joy in Incheon, where South Korea was playing, and 115 miles

away in Daejeon, where the U.S. was playing. The eventual 1-0 win put South Korea through, knocked out Portugal, and pulled the U.S. through as well.

Why did the United States Soccer Federation continue to encourage FIFA to play the 1986 World Cup in the U.S. long after FIFA had chosen Columbia to host it?
The worst-kept secret of international soccer in 1982 was that Columbia was having trouble preparing for the 1986 World Cup even though FIFA had already awarded it to that nation. The U.S., Brazil, and Mexico were working behind the scenes to get in line should Columbia bow out. In October Columbia officially withdrew as host, the first country to ever do that, setting up a competition among nations in the Western Hemisphere, since FIFA would be looking for one of them to take on the task. (Traditionally, FIFA alternated between Europe and the America's to host the World Cup.) Canada then entered the mix and eventually joined in a combined bid with the U.S. FIFA, facing a threatened boycott by South American nations if the tournament was moved north of Mexico, gave the 1986 tournament to Mexico.

On what date did the United States play Brazil in the 1994 World Cup?
Every nation that had hosted the World Cup prior to 1994 had qualified for the second round of the tournament. By winning one game and tying another among its first three matches, the United States managed to keep the string alive. The date for the U.S.'s knock-out game against Brazil inspired tournament organizers to request fireworks. A FIFA official responded, "There will be no fireworks." There were no fireworks for the U.S. on that July 4th as Brazil won 1-0. Exactly five years later and on the same field, Stanford Stadium, the two countries' women's teams faced each other in the 1999 Women's World Cup

semifinal. The U.S. won 2-0 and headed to the final
against China.

**What big announcement came from FIFA on July 4,
1988?**
Facing bids from the United States, Morocco, and Brazil,
the FIFA Executive Committee voted on that date to play
the 1994 World Cup in the United States.

More Goals

Who is the all-time career leader in goals for the NASL?
Your guess of Pele is so far off. He played only two-and-a-
half seasons in the league, scoring 31 goals in 56 games.
That's good enough for 92nd on the all-time list. Ninety-
one places ahead of him is Georgia Chinaglia, who came
into the league in 1976 and kept playing through 1983.
During those eight seasons, all with the Cosmos, Chinaglia
played in 213 games, scoring 193 goals.

**How many seasons did Georgia Chinaglia lead the
NASL in goals?**
Even though he played just 19 games of a 24-game season,
Chinaglia led the league in goals in 1976, his first year in
the NASL. He won the goal-scoring crown again in 1978,
1980, 1981, and 1982.

**In international competition, who has scored the most
goals?**
There are so many reasons that Mia Hamm was the most
recognized female athlete in the world. For three different
decades she was leading the team that was winning the
world's highest women's team competitions while she
appeared on Nike commercials and magazine covers and
overwhelmed people with charm, modesty, and good looks.

However, there's a number that gives credence to all that attention: 158. Hamm did not score until her 17th game with the U.S. Women's National Team, but when she retired in 2004, she had scored 158. It's a record that likely will stand for some time among women. The next active player is Kristine Lilly, a former teammate of Hamm, with 117 goals at the end of 2006. The next three places are occupied by retired players.

The man who has scored more international goals than any other man crossed paths with the United States Men's National Team. Who did he play for and when did those paths meet?
It was possibly the only bright spot of the Unites States' experience of the 1998 World Cup. The Americans prevented Ali Daei from scoring when they played Iran. Daei, at the end of 2006, was at 109 international goals and was still playing at 36 years old. His total goals in international competition was and still is above all other men.

Who holds the record for most professional career goals?
In addition to his club games, the Brazilian scored 97 times for his country, giving Pele a total of 1,281 goals. He scored them during 1,363 international and domestic league matches.

What are the most goals scored in a single game by one person for the United States Women's National Team?
During the qualifying phase of the 1991 Women's World Cup, Brandi Chastain came on as a substitute for Michelle Akers against Mexico and scored five times before the final whistle, ending a 12-0 win for the U.S. It surpassed any one-game mark by other U.S. women and men. Since then, the record of five goals in one game has been tied but never

broken. Seven months after Chastain's feat, Akers scored five goals against Taiwan during the 1991 World Cup. In 2002 Tiffeny Milbrett scored three in the first nine minutes of a game against Panama. She added two more before the match ended 9-0. Finally came Abby Wombach. She scored every U.S. goals in a 5-0 win against Ireland in 2004. All of hers came during the second half. The last one crossed the line in the 90th minute.

What are the most goals scored in a single game by one person for the United States Men's National Team?
In his first game for the United States Men's National Team, on November 8, 1925, Archie Stark scored four goals against Canada in a 6-1 victory. Stark stood alone for nine years but today shares the record for most goals in one U.S. men's game with Aldo (Buff) Donelli, Landon Donovan, and Joe-Max Moore. Donovan is the most recent player to score four in one match, versus Cuba in July 2003. Donelli scored his four in a 1934 game when the U.S. needed a win to be admitted to the World Cup. Facing Mexico, Donelli scored all of them, leading the U.S. to a 4-2 victory and sending the Mexicans back across the Atlantic. He could have earned sole possession of the record had he converted the easiest of shots. Donelli missed a penalty kick and the chance to finish with five goals. Joe-Max Moore scored four times on December 5, 1993, in the U.S.'s 7-0 win over El Salvador in Los Angeles. Like Donelli had with a penalty kick, Moore also had a legitimate opportunity to finish the game with five goals to his credit. According to *The U.S. Tackles the World Cup*, Moore actually scored what would have been his fifth, but the ball slipped through a hole in the net, and the referees ruled that the ball had gone wide of the goal.

Of the men who have played for the U.S. National Team, which has scored the most goals for the team?

His first game with the U.S. Men's National Team was in 1990, the start of a national team career that had him scoring at least one goal per year for 11 straight years. Among his record 34 goals for the team was the first goal for the United States in the 1994 World Cup. With the U.S. behind 1-0 to Switzerland, Eric Wynalda sent a 35-yard free kick into the net, helping the team reach the second phase of the tournament.

How long did it take Eddie Johnson to score in his first appearance for the U.S. Men's National Team?
Playing against El Salvador in a World Cup qualifier on October 9, 2004, Johnson came on as a substitute in the 71st minute. He scored a goal within four minutes.

How many minutes of playing time did Eddie Johnson need to score his first four international goals?
He played 20 minutes during his first appearance, scoring once. Against Panama three days later, Johnson came on as a substitute in the 65th minute and scored during minutes 70, 84, and 87, becoming the first member of the U.S. Men's National Team to score a hat trick as a substitute. His total of four goals was scored during only 43 minutes of playing time. A fluke? Only slightly. Something inside Coach Bruce Arena said, Maybe I should start Eddie Johnson. So Johnson started against Jamaica, played 88 minutes and scored another goal. Getting a start against Trinidad and Tobago, Johnson scored in the 30th minute, giving him six goals in 154 minutes on the field and four straight games with at least one goal in each.

Through 2006 how many people other than Johnson have scored for the U.S. in four straight national team appearances?
William Looby completed it in 1955, and Brian McBride tied him in 2001. They are the only other two. Looby's

string started in January 1954 and ended in August 1955. McBride's streak started with a match against Mexico in June 2000, included two more matches that year, and concluded in January 2001 against China.

Through ten seasons, who is the all-time career leader in goals for the MLS?

Through 2006 Jason Kries had 31 game-winning goals. He finished the 2006 season with a career of 108 goals. With 18 goals in 1999, he was voted the league MVP. Also, he has played for the U.S. Men's National team 14 times.

Through 2006 what's the record for most goals in one MLS season?

Playing for the Tampa Bay Mutiny, Roy Lassiter scored 25 minutes into the team's first game during MLS's first season. He went on to score 26 more in 1996. Through the season, Lassiter had only one hat-trick and twice scored in six consecutive games.

What are the most goals scored by one player in an MLS game and who scored them?

His team, the New York/New Jersey MetroStars, gave up four goals on Aug. 26, 2000, so Clint Mathis chose the correct game to score five alone. His first one came in the third minute from his left foot. The second was a simple tap in from a rebound. After Dallas scored once, Mathis put a right footer into the net before Dallas scored three times. Two minutes later Mathis scored his fourth. He put his team ahead for good with a penalty kick in the 78th minute. At the time of Mathis's feat, Raul Diaz Arce was the only player to have scored four times in a game. Arce has done it twice.

Who leads the MetroStars/Red Bulls in career goals?

Giovanni Savarese scored in the MetroStars' first game in

team history, in April 1996. Through the season, he never gave up the club's goal-scoring lead and finished 1996 with 13 goals. At the end of his third season, his last with the team, he had 41 goals, the career most. Through the 2006 season nobody else has scored as many for the team, meaning that he has led the team since his first game and the team's first game.